HINTS FOR
HASSLE-FREE LIVING WITH....
Kids

HINTS FOR
HASSLE-FREE LIVING WITH....
Kids

BARBARA BRIDDOCK

SALLY MILNER PUBLISHING

First published in 1991 by
Sally Milner Publishing Pty Ltd
17 Wharf Road
Birchgrove NSW 2041 Australia

Production by Sylvana Scannapiego, Island Graphics
Design by Doric Order
Illustrations by Robert Freeman
Author photograph by Judith Hogg
Typeset in Australia by Asset Typesetting Pty Ltd
Printed in Australia by The Book Printer

National Library of Australia
Cataloguing-in-Publication data:

Briddock, Barbara.
    Hints for hassle-free living with kids.

    Includes index.
    ISBN 1 86351 026 5.

    1. Child-rearing. I. Title.

649.1

Distributed in Australia by Transworld Publishers

To my two very precious daughters Laura and Emily
To their beloved daddy David Briddock
And to their special grand-dad Bob Eccles
This book is lovingly dedicated.

Acknowledgements

My thanks to Jo Brock, Sarah Cammell, Dr Robyn Coulson, Rachel Denning, Sally Gibbings, Zita Horton, Harry McCay, Meryl McCay, Honara Taufahema, Deborah Watson and Rebecca Watson. Thanks also to my friends, who through their example have given me many of the ideas in this book.

Special thanks to Robert Freeman for his illustrations.

Contents

Introduction   1

1. Hassle-Free Living with Kids At Play   3
Adult Involvement; Babies; Baking; Balls; Bicycles; Blackboards and Chalk; Board Games; Books and Stories; Brooms; Bubble-Blowing; Building Blocks and Constructions; Butterfly Catching; Card Games; Carving; Collages; Collections; Colouring-In; Coordination Games; Crayons; Crossword Puzzles; Dens and Huts; Dolls; Drawing; Dressing-Up; Growing Things; Hammering; Jigsaw Puzzles; Lego; Listening Games; Masks; Memory Games; Mobiles; Music; Outside Play; Paddling Pools; Painting; Papier Mâché; Paste; Play Dough; Play Mat; Playpens; Pole Tennis; Posting; Puppets, Roller Skates; Sandpits; Sewing; Shaving Cream Fun; Shops; Slides; Speech Games; Stilts; Swimming; Swings; Threading; Touching Games; Toys; Trampolines; Water Play.

2. Hassle-Free Living with Kids in the Bathroom   38
Bathing Baby; Bath Toys; Children in the Bath; Dangerous Objects and Substances; Electricity; Hot-Water; Locks; Planning a New Bathroom; Slipping; Toilets.

3. Hassle-Free Living with Kids in the Bedroom   45
Babies in Bed; Bedrooms; Children in Beds; Cold Weather; Hot Weather; Sick Children in Bed.

4. Hassle-Free Living With Kids and their Clothes   57
Aprons; Baby Clothes; Belts; Bibs; Booties; Bows; Buttons; Cold Weather; Dresses; Dressing Babies and Toddlers; Dressing in the Mornings; Gloves and Mittens; Hand-Me-Downs; Hanging Clothes; Hems; Jeans; Knitting for Children; Long Pants; Name Tags; Overalls, Crawlers; Nappies; Plastic Pants; Pyjamas and Nighties; Raincoats; Sewing Children's Clothes; Shawls; Shirts and Blouses; Shoes; Singlets; Skirts; Socks; Sun Hats; Uniforms; Washing Children's Clothes; Woollens; Zips.

5. Hassle-Free Living with Kids' Development 78

Bad Habits; Crying; Dummies; Fears; Independence; Irritable Children; Keys; Kindergarten; Left and Right; Listening; Manners; Matches; Money; Problem Solving; Reminders; Security Blankets; Sharing; Shopping; Speech; Teething; Telephones; Thumb-sucking; Time; Toilet Training.

6. Hassle-Free Living with Kids in Families 90

Communication; Family Activities; Family Rules; Family Nights; Fathers; Fighting; Mementos; Mothers; Moving House; Photographs; Self-Esteem; Sibling Rivalry; Special Time; Television; When Daddy or Mummy Goes Away.

7. Hassle-Free Living with Kids' Grooming 109

Appearance; Fingernails; Glasses; Hair Accessories; Hair Cutting; Hair Washing; Jewellery; Teeth.

8. Hassle-Free Living with Kids on Holiday 115

Beach; Bed Time; Belongings; Camp Fires; Camping; Cooking; Overseas Holidays; Packing for Holidays; Picnics; Sun; Tents; Tramping and Walking; Washing.

9. Hassle-Free Living with Kids at Meal Times 122

Baby Food Jars; Barbecues; Bibs; Bottles; Breakfast; Breastfeeding; Children in the Kitchen; Drinking; Eating; Feeding Babies; Health-Consciousness; Highchairs; Lunches; Meal Times; Microwaves; Overweight Children; Plastic Food Containers; Reluctant and Slow Eaters; School Lunches; Self-Feeding; Tablecloths; Individual Foods; Bread, Cereals, Eggs, Fruit, Honey, Ice Cream, Ice Cream Cones, Jellies, Milk Shakes, Popcorn, Sandwiches, Soup, Vegetables, Yoghurt.

10. Hassle-Free Living with Kids on Outings 140

Babysitters; Be Prepared; Crowded Places; Movies; Restaurants; Shopping; Stranger Danger; Strollers; Suggestions for Outings; Visiting; Walks.

11. Hassle-Free Living with Kids at School 150

Belongings; Bookmark; Books; Bus Fares; Calculators; Certificates; Computers; Desks; Felt-Tipped Pens; Flowers for the Teacher; Glue; Homework; Ink; Insects for School; Labels; Lunch Boxes and Bottles; Money; Notes for the Teacher; Paper; Parents' Involvement in School; Pencils; Posters; Preparing Children for School; Projects; Rubbers; Rulers; School Bags; School Books; School Mornings; School Photographs; Scissors; Starting School; Sticky Tape; Travelling to School.

12. Hassle-Free Living with Kids on Special Occasions 163
Arrival of a Baby; Birthday Parties; Christmas; Easter; Greeting Cards.

13. Hassle-Free Living with Kids in Transit 176
Air Travel; Bus Travel; Car Travel; Games and Activities for Children.

14. Hassle-Free Living with Kids at Work 191
Attitude to Work; Bathroom; Bed-Making; Bedrooms; Cooking; Dishwashing; Dusting; Enlisting Helpers; Fruit-Picking; Helpfulness; Ironing; Rewards; Rosters; Shoe Cleaning; Table-Setting; Tidiness; Time Limits; Toddler's Helpfulness; Toys; Washing.

Index 203

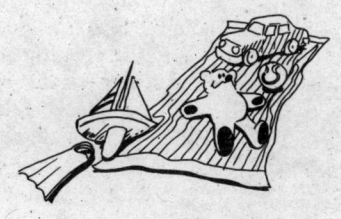

Introduction

Last Armistice Day, my husband, David, had been looking after the children for most of the morning. Remembering what day it was I remarked, 'We should have two minutes silence at 11.00 am' (a practice which seems to have died out, but which we adhered to at school, on the eleventh day of the eleventh month at eleven o'clock, to remember the servicemen who died in the First World War). David's response to my suggestion was 'That will be wonderful!' I am sure it wasn't the servicemen he had in mind so much, nor was he feeling particularly patriotic at the time, but the thought of two minutes silence, after looking after a baby and a two-year-old for a few hours, was simply delightful . . . roll on November!

For all you mums and dads who enjoyed the freedom of being single, or married without children, and for those who remember what it was like to sleep all through the night, to eat your dinner while it was still hot, to read the newspaper in peace and to be able to jump in and out of the car without feeling like a mule laden down with every conceivable 'just-in-case' — welcome to the real world . . . of kids!

Hassle-free Living With Kids, is not a novel! Although hassle-free living seems impossible with children, few of us would be without them!

So next time world peace is threatened by the way the sandwiches were cut into triangles instead of rectangles, remember that the medal you think you deserve for surviving, is standing in front of you, holding a plate of triangle-shaped sandwiches, made soggy with tears!

Before your child becomes a teenager, there will be approximately 2600 sandwiches to cut, 8760 teeth-brushing sessions, 5110 nappies to change, 3120 baths to run, 1400 school mornings to survive, 8736 changes of clothes and several thousands of dollars spent on housekeeping. And that is just with one child! No wonder we are encouraged to take one day at a time! However, this book is full of ideas to help save time, money and problems in these everyday situations with children.

To make the book easy to follow, the headings and subheadings are generally in alphabetical order, except when chronological order is more logical. Ideas on recycling are scattered throughout the book. Look at the index for a list of useful things to keep.

I suggest you read the book through, so as to give you an idea of its contents, and then keep it handy to refer to regularly. Next time there is something specific you are planning, such as a holiday or birthday party, next time the children are bored or when you feel like some extra inspiration for the regular tasks such as feeding children and putting them to bed, read again the appropriate section, to give you some great ideas on how to make the time more 'hassle-free'. And why not set aside a little time once a week in the evening, after the children have gone to bed, to prepare an activity or game from the At Play chapter, for your children to enjoy the next day. It will be worth the small amount of organisation on your part to see them involved and thoroughly enjoying a different activity.

So all those of you who will benefit from some brainwaves for your baby, tips for your toddler, ideas for infants, clues for children or even some recommendations for rascals — this book was written for you. May it be an inspiration to you and the means to help enhance your family in its times of celebrations, difficulties, routines, work and play.

God bless!

Barbara

HASSLE-FREE LIVING WITH KIDS...
At play

(see also **HOLIDAYS** *and* **IN TRANSIT***)*

ADULT INVOLVEMENT

An adult's involvement in a child's play should seldom be one of an 'adviser'. It is important for children to learn from experimenting and experience rather than to always have an adult tell them 'how to make the man stand up in the sand'. Play along *with* the child, rather than *above* him, so that he is not always left feeling like the inferior one.

To encourage a child to play a particular game or play with a puzzle or toy that he doesn't seem particularly interested in, sit down and play with it yourself! Chances are, he will want to join in.

BABIES

To protect a newborn baby from toddlers who are playing nearby, place her on a rug or in a baby seat in a playpen. She will be able to see what is going on without being trampled on or loved too vigorously!

To prevent a crawling baby spoiling an older child's game, place the older child and his blocks or toys in the playpen away from harm's way!

If you need to put a baby in a playpen outside, secure it to the ground with tent pegs to stop baby moving it.

Babies' Toys (see also IN THE BEDROOM chapter)

To keep a baby amused:
— fill an old, clean pillowcase with cellophane. Sew up the end and he will enjoy the crackling noise as he plays with it;

— cut one leg off a pair of old, clean pantyhose and fill it with soft clean paper or cellophane. Tie the end up before giving it to baby to play with;

— place a non-breakable mirror in baby's cot or bassinet;

— keep old plastic hair rollers for baby to roll around and stack inside each other. Make sure they have no loose pieces.

BAKING (see also Cooking in AT WORK chapter)

Young children love to 'help' you when you are cooking in the kitchen. Try to let them join in, but if what you are doing is dangerous or too difficult, supply them with a plastic bowl, a wooden spoon and some flour and water to mix up 'for you'. Many late afternoon crises can be averted if children are given the opportunity to be assistant chef!

While cooking in the kitchen, give your child the ingredients to make **baker's clay.** They can mix together 2 cups plain flour, with 1 cup salt and 1 cup water. This will require kneading for about ten minutes and then can be moulded into shape and baked for one hour at 180°C. It can be painted and varnished when cool.

From the very beginning, encourage children **to be organised and careful in the kitchen when they are cooking.** Before they start cooking, they should check that:
— their hands are clean;

— long hair is tied back;

— they have an apron on;

— there is sufficient clear working space for them;

— they have read the recipe through so they know what ingredients, methods and time will be required to make it up;

— they have arranged all the ingredients on the bench;

— the oven is set at the correct temperature;

— they have filled the sink, or a large bowl, with warm water so that each utensil can be placed in to soak as soon as it is finished with, to save a lot of time washing up later.

To prevent children adding too much food colouring to icing:
— put a few drops of food colouring into an empty essence bottle. Add enough water to dilute the colouring to an acceptable shade, so that if a few too many drops are added, it will not make the icing too psychedelic!

— dip a skewer into the bottle and allow the colouring to drip into the mixture.

If your children want to help with icing a cake, they can press different shaped biscuit cutters into the icing while it is soft and colour in the outlines with icing of a contrasting colour. They will enjoy colouring in the animal and heart shapes.

To save the time taken to ice cup cakes, children can simply put a chocolate button, chocoate sprinkles or half a marshmallow on top of the cake when it is cooked and then put it back in the oven for a couple of minutes to allow it to melt.

To keep the recipe book clean and in good order when children are cooking, open it and place it inside a clear plastic bag, so the directions can be seen.

BALLS (see also Swimming, this chapter)

Give a nylon net ball to baby to play with. It is light and won't hurt ornaments if it is thrown in the wrong direction.

To make a soft ball from old socks, fold the first two socks in the normal manner, bringing the ribbed top tightly over to form a small ball. Then, use one sock each time to roll tightly around the previous ones, bringing the ribbed top firmly over. Stitch the last one firmly to hold it together.

When first teaching a child to catch a ball, use a balloon. It will move more slowly, allowing extra time for the child to catch it and children love to play with balloons (see Balloon Safety, in ON SPECIAL OCCASIONS chapter).

To carry a large ball to school or to a picnic, give your child a string bag to put it in. This is especially good if they ride a bicycle to school.

Use scraps of plumbers' PVC pipe, for children to roll balls through.

BEADS *(see* Threading, *this chapter)*

BICYCLES

If your children ride on your driveway too close to the road, paint a 'Stop' line across the drive at a safe distance from the road. Tell them that they must not cross the line.

If your children have to leave their bikes out in the rain at times, get them to take a shower cap with them to place over the seat, to keep it dry.

To remove surface rust from a bicycle, rub over the metal with a silver milk bottle top.

BLACKBOARDS AND CHALK

To keep chalks together, put them in a soap box.

To give more room to keep chalks and dusters, attach a tray to both sides of the easel at the bottom of the blackboard.

To keep chalk in long pieces and to keep children's hands clean while using coloured chalk, wrap sticky tape around the pieces before giving them to children to use. The tape can be unwound as required.

For a different use for blackboards, stand a blackboard up outside, give your child a container of water and a paintbrush and let him paint to his heart's content. Each picture will dry after a few minutes and he can start again.

To make a blackboard:
— paint a piece of smooth board with blackboard paint;
— paint an old roller blind with blackboard paint. Hang it in your children's play area or on a veranda and it can be rolled up out of the way when not in use.

One way to redirect the talents of your secret 'wall scribbler' is to paint an area of suitable wall with blackboard paint. Children are then told that this is the only wall available to them. Once they pass this stage, the wall can be simply painted over with a fresh coat of paint.

BOARD GAMES

To make it easier for children to play board games, place the board on a lazy Susan in the middle of the table and then no-one needs to play 'upside down'!

To make a board game last longer:
— varnish over the cardboard;

— cover it with clear, self-adhesive vinyl.

Keep the manufacturer's instructions for all the board games pasted into one exercise book for future reference.

Toothpaste tops of various colours can be cleaned and used to play board games.

BOOKS AND STORIES (see also AT SCHOOL chapter)

Because young children have a limited attention span, it is important to **make the reading sessions enjoyable and the stories very interesting.** Do this by:
— giving the child your full attention while reading him a story;

— don't rush through the story;

— use different voices to dramatise the story;

— choose some books with special little surprises in them, such as flaps to lift up and pop-up pictures;

— read stories which have repetition and stop occasionally for your child to finish off the word or line;

— read lots of humorous books that you can laugh at together;

— read books with lots of rhyming and rhythm so the children can really get involved;

— when reading well-known books, occasionally change something in the story to see if your child picks it up, e.g. in the story of the Gingerbread man, see if you are corrected when saying 'Run, run as slow as you can, you can't catch me I'm the Gingerbread man'.

To make an ideal 'first book' for children:
— take your own photographs of things that are familiar to your baby, such as teddy bear, cot, daddy, sister, telephone, highchair etc. Use a cheap, plastic photograph album to display these and write captions on paper to slip in with the photo. If you want to make several books, divide them up into different subjects, such as toys, family and friends, food we eat, things to feel etc.;

— fill a small, cheap, plastic photograph album with bright pictures cut from magazines, postcards, pictures from greeting cards and photographs of familiar people and animals. The plastic will make the book washable and the pictures can be replaced with others for extra variety.

To encourage babies and toddlers to read books:
— leave little stacks of baby books around the house in places your baby visits on his travels. If they are within his reach, he is likely to pick them up and enjoy them before moving on to the next place. Even magazines and junk mail provide him with 'reading' material;

— leave some books in his cot for him to look at when he wakes up. These should preferably be 'baby-proof' books which have plastic or cardboard pages. A child who can stand could have some left in a basket hanging over the side of his cot;

— tell him stories from family photograph albums.

If you don't seem to get time to read for your own pleasure, with a new baby, sit him on your knee or rock him while reading your own book or newspaper aloud. He will enjoy your voice, while you enjoy the story.

To add variety to your child's book-reading activities, and to keep him amused while you are busy, make up audio cassettes of different stories that your children can listen to while following the story in a book. Don't forget to signal when it is time for them to turn the pages. **If grandparents cannot see the children regularly,** why not suggest that they make up story tapes as well. The children will enjoy nanna reading to them, even though she is not there. This is also a good idea **if mummy or daddy has to go away from home for a while.**

WARNING: Make sure toddlers and babies cannot get their hands on cassette tapes, which they can easily undo and wrap around their bodies and perhaps their necks – not to mention the damage that could be done to your favourite opera! If a child is not closely supervised, make sure he cannot reach the tape.

If your child tends to choose the same story each time, add a little variety by writing down the names of all his favourite stories on separate pieces of paper and putting them all in a box. At story time, he can choose a piece of paper from the 'Lucky Dip', which will have a title on it.

To make it easier to afford to have books available for your children:
— buy them at school fetes and fairs. They are often sold very cheaply at closing time;

— save up some money to spend at your city's library sale. Although the books sold are usually not in perfect condition, the fact that they have been bound and covered for use in the library means that there is usually still a lot of life left in them.

If your children tear their books:
— do not take away their privilege to read books. Even though tearing books is to be discouraged, your punishment could be too permanent if you don't let them look at books at all;

— give them old or second hand books to read by themselves. They could be inexpensively replaced at the next school or church fete;

— keep their good books aside for them to read when you are with them.

To repair torn books, cover the pages with clear, self-adhesive vinyl. This will make them stronger and easily kept clean.

Make audio cassettes of children's stories read on radio and television. Children will enjoy listening to these in the car especially.

BROOMS

Keep your children's play broom when they have finished with it. They are great to use, with a pan, for sweeping up things without having to bend down too much.

BUBBLE-BLOWING

Try the following bubble-blowing mixtures:
— mix $1/2$ cup bubble bath, or good quality dishwashing detergent, with $1/3$ cup hot water and leave it to stand for about eight hours, until it becomes a syrup. Add a few drops of glycerine to the mixture;

— mix a solution made from baby shampoo and water with one teaspoon glycerine. If the mixture gets into a child's eyes, it should not hurt too much if you use baby shampoo.

To make up bubble-blowing mixture that will last indefinitely, boil several small pieces of soap in 600 mls water for about five minutes. When cool, add a tablespoon of glycerine. Keep it airtight and use as required.

To blow bubbles, use:
— a piece of twisted wire;

— the hole in a cotton reel;

— a pipe cleaner, twisted into a round shape;

— a straw. Only allow older children to use straws, when you can be sure they will blow and not suck the mixture!

To make multi-coloured bubbles, use several different bowls of detergent with a different food colouring in each.

BUILDING BLOCKS AND CONSTRUCTIONS
(see also **Lego,** *this chapter)*

To make light building blocks for very young children, cut large blocks out of foam rubber. Thick pieces of foam rubber can be cut easily with scissors. They are preferable to heavy wooden blocks.

Save some of the following items for children to **use for building constructions:** margarine and yoghurt pots; cardboard wine casks; egg cartons; matchboxes; PVC plumbing pipe (makes a great tunnel); tea bag boxes; cardboard tubes; bottle tops; cotton reels; plastic lids.

BUTTERFLY CATCHING

Use old tennis racket frames to make into butterfly catchers. Sew a cloth bag or net on the frame and the children should get a lot of enjoyment and exercise! Badminton and squash rackets can be used as well.

CARD GAMES

Replace the cardboard box that cards come in with a plastic soap box, when it gets ruined.

To keep card games in good condition, if they are used frequently, cover with clear, self-adhesive vinyl.

CAR GAMES *(see* IN TRANSIT *chapter)*

CARVING

To make a soap carving, older children simply need a cake of soap and a small vegetable knife. Adult supervision should be given until you are confident that your child is mature enough to handle the knife carefully.

To teach a left-handed person how to carve, show them what you are doing in the mirror. If you are left-handed and are showing a right-handed person, use the mirror also.

COLLAGES

Collect the following for making collages: greeting cards, coloured paper, stamps, foil, pieces of fabric, wool, ribbon, milk bottle tops, pasta, cotton wool, tissue paper, string, scraps of paper, feathers, leaves, sticks, flowers etc.

Store all the collage materials in separate containers, so that they will all be in reasonable order when your children come to use it. Small items can be kept in the compartments of egg cartons, while larger amounts of things can be kept in margarine or yoghurt containers with lids.

Try some of the following collage ideas with your children:
— get them to make a 'feely collage', by pasting all sorts of bits and pieces with different textures, on to a large sheet of cardboard, e.g. sand, seeds, cotton wool, sawdust, playdough, upside down sticky tape, rope, bark, rice, stone etc.

— draw a self-portrait and cover it with all sorts of bits and pieces that look like hair, skin, eyes, mouth etc.

COLLECTIONS
Shell Collections
Display shell collections:
— on a large tray. Use plasticine to hold the shell on the tray;

— in a shirt box, with a clear lid.

Keep special shells in the individual dividers of an egg carton.

Use large, flat shells, which your children have collected, to make soap dishes.

Stamp Collecting
While waiting to assemble stamps in an album, keep them in an old money box.

To remove stamps easily from an envelope, put it in the freezer for a couple of hours and then lift the stamp off with tweezers.

COLOURING-IN (see Crayons, this chapter)
To make inexpensive colouring-in books, give a child an outdated volume of the Yellow Pages telephone book.

COORDINATION GAMES
Fine Motor Skills (see also Threading, this chapter)
To help your little ones develop strength in their fingers:
— give her one bowl of plain water and two smaller bowls of water coloured with food colouring. With a medicine dropper, she can suck up some of the coloured water and drop it into the clear water. Not only will her fingers be exercised, but she will be able to see what happens when two colours are mixed together;

— give them some spring pegs to play with. Either set up a 'clothesline' at their height or give them a basket handle or empty milk powder can to clip the pegs on to;

— give her a bowl of uncooked pasta, kidney beans, acorns or uncracked nuts and melon baller or spoon and another bowl. Get her to see how many she can pick up and put into the other bowl without dropping any. She could then try it with a pair of tongs.

Pouring Drinks

To teach your child to pour drinks from a jug, let them practise with a jug containing rice or split peas. Show them how to hold the handle with one hand and use the other hand to support the bottom of the jug.

CRAYONS *(see also* Colouring-in, *this chapter)*

To keep crayons tidy, put them in a soap container. They will not easily break and will be more difficult for baby brothers and sisters to get hold of.

To sharpen crayons, dip the ends in hot water and then roll them to a point between your thumb and forefinger.

To make soap crayons, which will easily wipe off walls, floors and bodies, mix one eighth cup water with three quarters cup soap flakes until it is thoroughly mixed into a thick paste. Divide it up to add different food colourings and press the mixture into an ice cube tray. Allow it to dry out in a warm place for a couple of days.

CROSSWORD PUZZLES

If your children enjoy doing crossword puzzles, cut them out of the children's pages of magazines and newspapers, along with their solutions, and paste them into a scrap book for them to do on a rainy day or when they are sick.

DENS AND HUTS

To make a temporary den or hut:
— hang a curtain or piece of fabric around a sturdy change table, so that your older children will enjoy playing in their little cubby house with their dolls and toys while you change baby's nappies. The light, fold-up change tables would not be suitable;

— drape an old sheet or preferably a bedspread over a table or strong clotheshorse. (Sheets may allow too much light to penetrate this secret hiding place!);

— peg an old bedspread or tarpaulin on to the clothesline so that it hangs down to the ground. Use nails or small stakes to secure the ends of it to the ground;

— use several chairs to fence off the corner of a room and cover with a blanket. Toys can have new appeal to children in their very own territory;

— drape an old bedspread or large blanket over an old wooden playpen.

To make a more permanent 'hut':
— sew a piece of canvas or cloth all the way around the edge of a beach umbrella;

— make a proper little 'house', out of strong fabric or canvas, to sit over the dining room table. An old tablecloth or sheet could be used as a starting point, to cover the table and from which to sew on the four walls that will hang down. Cut out a door and a window or two. To make it look decorative, paint the walls, paint a flower box and flowers under the window and some flowers 'growing up' against the bottom of the house. This is great to take out on a wet day for the children to play 'house' in, with their toys and friends.

— decorate a huge cardboard box, the type that large home appliances come in. Cut out holes for windows and doors. It can be painted and furnished inside.

DOLLS

To clean dolls' faces, rub over the face with a cotton ball soaked in astringent lotion.

To brighten up the face of a china doll, paint a coat of clear nail polish over it.

To remove felt-tipped pen from dolls' faces, rub with nail polish remover.

Dolls' Clothes and Accessories

Keep some of your babies' tiny clothes for your children to use as dolls' clothes later on.

Make dolls' clothes from the fabric in old, discarded clothes.

A good time to make dolls' clothes is when you are sewing other garments. Use the scraps to cut out small garments and sew them while the sewing machine is threaded and set up for that fabric.

To make inexpensive buttons for dolls' clothes, use a paper punch to cut tiny circles out of plastic lids. Use a hot needle to poke holes through the 'buttons' to sew them on with.

Use sock hangers to make hangers for dolls' clothes. They will fit perfectly in a 'wardrobe' made from a shoe box.

Dolls' House Accessories

To make holders for dolls' miniature cookies, use the tiny crimped 'cup cake papers' from chocolate boxes.

Let your children do the 'washing up' with their dolls' tea sets. Give them a bowl, dish brush and tea towel and allow them to have fun, while gaining experience in washing and drying dishes, preferably outside!

DRAWING

To encourage small children to draw, start drawing a picture yourself and leave a few simple details for the child to fill in, e.g. the whiskers on a cat, the door on a house, the sun in the sky etc.

Play the game, 'Blindfolded Artists'. One person is blindfolded and is given a pencil and paper or piece of chalk and blackboard. Another person asks her to try to draw something without looking, e.g. a house or a cat. The children have to expect a lot of laughs as they draw the door of the house on the roof or the cat's whiskers on its tail!

DRESSING-UP

Children love to dress up and they love to look at themselves when they do so. Keep a large mirror in your child's play room or bedroom so she can look at herself while dressing up. Children can be kept amused for a long time by simply having a mirror to look into.

Collect the following items for your child's dressing-up wardrobe: beads, belts, berets, bow ties, braces, curtains (to use as capes and cloaks), evening dresses, feathers, glasses, gloves, hats, handbags, jewellery, pantyhose, scarves, shawls, shoes (little girls prefer high heels), ties, veils, waistcoats, walking sticks, wigs etc.

GROWING THINGS

To encourage a child to develop his own little garden, allocate a small area for him to plant flowers or vegetable seeds. Weeding, watering and looking after the plants should develop in him a sense of responsibility and give him a great sense of achievement when he sees them growing and when he can pick a bunch of flowers and eat some of his vegetables.

To make an attractive climbing plant, fill a milk bottle with water and poke a sweet potato in the top so it is just touching the water. Before long, roots will appear and the sweet potato will sprout leaves.

To make a cress man, put some cotton wool in an empty half eggshell and paint the face of a man on the shell. Dampen the cotton wool and sprinkle some cress seeds over it. After a few days the seeds will sprout and produce a crop of hair on the cress man's head. Keep the cotton wool moist all the time.

To make a cress animal, join two or three potatoes together with toothpicks or match sticks to form the animal of your choice. Give it match-stick legs and ears and a tail, and carve or paint a face with felt-tip pens. Using a match stick, poke out little holes all over the top of the animal's body and head and poke cress or mustard seeds into the holes. It should not take too many days for the animal to be covered with 'hair'.

To germinate seeds, use half egg-shells placed in an egg carton. Fill them with soil and the seed and when the seedlings are ready to plant, crack the bottom of the shell to free the roots.

To show children how flowers and plants drink, stand a piece of celery, a white flower on a stem and a piece of carrot, with its bottom cut off, in a glass of water to which has been added some food colouring. Cut into the celery and the carrot to see the colour change. The flower will be more obvious.

HAMMERING

To reduce the risk of injury when children are learning to hammer nails:
— hold the nail on the piece of wood with play dough or plasticine, rather than little fingers;
— poke the nail through a piece of thin cardboard and hold the edge of the cardboard while hammering in the nail, before tearing it away;
— put a little oil or grease on the tip of the nail first, to make it drive through the wood more easily.

JIGSAW PUZZLES

To make inexpensive jigsaw puzzles:
— stick pictures or enlarged photographs of people or pets, that the

children know, on to cardboard. Cut the cardboard into interesting shapes for the children to join together. If you have a real jigsaw (a saw which can follow curved and wiggly lines), a more permanent puzzle can be made by gluing the pictures on to very heavy card or thin plywood;

— paste pictures from calendars, postcards and posters on to cardboard and cut them into different shapes and sizes, according to the child's ability;

— cut up old greeting cards for an instant jigsaw puzzle.

When making jigsaw puzzles for very young children, if possible keep an identical picture complete for them to follow.

To help a child put together a difficult jigsaw puzzle, colour-code or number the backs of the pieces according to where they fit together. If he gets stuck, these codes may prevent him from becoming too frustrated and giving up.

When older children are working on a large jigsaw puzzle, keep it together on an old dinner wagon, which can be turned around to reach all the pieces and wheeled out of the way when not in use.

To store jigsaw puzzles, so pieces don't get lost:
— put each puzzle in its own ice cream container with its name and the number of pieces written on the lid;

— with a felt-tipped pen, paint a little spot on the back of each piece of the jigsaw. Use a different colour for each puzzle so that if they get mixed up they can easily be sorted;

LEGO (see Building Blocks, this chapter)

To store Lego, or other similar blocks, when you have large quantities, use several plastic cutlery trays. The Lego can be sorted into the different compartments in the trays, so that all the fences are kept in one section, all the wheels in another, the trees in another and so on. The trays can then be stacked on top of each other to be put away.

To clear away the Lego blocks quickly, use a plastic dust pan to scoop them up and place in the bucket or bag. A small one can be kept with the blocks for this purpose. If you still have difficulty getting children motivated, supply one shovel or scoop for each child and have a competition to see who can shovel up the blocks the fastest.

LISTENING GAMES (see also Listening in DEVELOPMENT chapter)

To develop children's listening skills, play the following games:
— stand several children in a long line. Whisper a short message

into the first child's ear. Have her whisper it into the next child's ear and so on down the line until the last one, who has to say it out loud to all the children. The final version can sometimes end up quite funny and very different from the original;

— poke a plastic funnel into each end of a piece of hose. Two people can use this as a telephone, with one person speaking into one funnel, while the other listens with her funnel up to her ear;

— play the game 'My aunt went to Paris and bought . . .' The first person says 'My aunt went to Paris and bought (e.g. a poodle) and then the next person says 'My aunt went to Paris and bought a poodle and (e.g. a sausage)'. The children need to concentrate to remember each item in order before adding their own idea;

— play 'What am I?' games, e.g. For a young child, it could be 'I am round, red or green on the outside and white in the middle. I have little pips inside my tummy and a stalk on top of my head.' Make them more difficult for an older child.

MASKS

To make a simple mask, use a large brown paper bag. Cut out eyes and mouths, paint faces on them and use cotton wool, fabric or wool for the hair.

MEMORY GAMES (see Listening Games, this chapter)

To exercise a child's memory, play some of the following games:
— Kim's Game. Set out a few objects on a tray for the child to look at for a short time. Cover the tray and see how many things she can remember. Adjust the number of objects and time allowed according to the age of the child;

— cut out pictures of people from old magazines and stick them on to cardboard. Show the child a picture for a few moments and then turn it over and the child has to remember what the person was wearing.

MOBILES (see also IN THE BEDROOM chapter)

Older children can make their own large mobiles to decorate the room:
— a cane or plastic hoop can be strung up to the ceiling and used to hang all sorts of decorative things from. Children can make colourful fish, animals, people and designs of any sort, using a wide variety of materials, to hang down from the hoop;

— a dry branch from a tree, about one metre in length, can be made into a mobile by hanging all sorts of decorations from it. The branch will look especially good if your children would like to make leaves, birds' nests and birds to hang from the branches.

MUSIC

Encourage your children to use everyday household items as musical instruments:
— cardboard tubes can be used as **'trumpets'**;

— plastic containers, mixing bowls or buckets can be turned upside down to use as **'drums'** with a piece of dowelling or a wooden spoon as a drum stick. Plastic containers will make quieter drums than coffee cans and pots and pans!

— a tissue box can be made into a **'banjo'**. Stretch different-sized rubber bands around the box, to be plucked;

— pot lids can be used as **'cymbals'** (sorry mums and dads!).

To make musical chimes, line up several milk bottles, all containing different amounts of water. Tap them with a stick and listen to the different notes produced by different bottles.

To make a pair of maracas, use two empty detergent bottles with handles. Put some lentils, rice or dried peas inside and glue the lid back on. Decorate the bottles if you wish. Use the handles to shake the bottles.

To encourage a love of music in your children:
— take an interest in people playing musical instruments. Talk about how the guitar is being 'strummed' or 'plucked', how the man is 'blowing' the trumpet and how the man is 'beating' the drum;

— make a conscious effort to sing, whistle and hum when you are with the children and encourage them to do the same;

— set aside time each day to sing a few songs together, perhaps after the story at bedtime;

— have music playing on a tape each night, in the child's bedroom. Playing music like this will often help to settle a crying baby also;

— make up little songs and rhymes about the activities and chores you are doing through the day.

To encourage your children to move and dance to music:
— play different styles of music and show the children how some music is suitable for galloping to, while another type suits swaying, another walking, running, skipping and so on. Give them plenty of opportunity to create other movements as they interpret the music provided;

— dance with the child sometimes and give them a few ideas of animals and birds etc, for them to imitate in their dancing;

— give the children scarves or sheets of paper to wave around while they are dancing or tie streamers to their wrists. Props like these can encourage more involvement in the dancing.

OUTSIDE PLAY
Chasing Shadows
Have fun playing outside, chasing each other's shadows. Instead of tagging the person, just jump on their shadow.

Hoops (see also Mobiles, this chapter)
Use hoops for the following games:
— place them on the ground and throw felt balls into them;

— hang a hoop from a tree and throw a ball through it;

— use a hoop to skip with instead of a rope;

— place several hoops on the ground for children to jump and hop into;

— use them as 'safe houses' when playing chasy, so that when you are inside the hoop you cannot be caught;

— roll the hoop from one person to another;

— hold them up for children to run through;

— use the hoop for 'hula hooping'.

Hot Weather
To make a shaded area for children to play in, peg a large sheet over the top of the clothes' line for the children to play underneath.

When children are playing outside in hot weather, leave plastic cups and a covered, plastic jug of water outside for them to help themselves. This will save them having to come panting into the house in their dirty clothes, requesting drinks.

When children are playing outside and need to know the time, put a clock in the window, facing out, so they won't have to keep running in and out to ask the time.

PADDLING POOLS (see also Swimming, this chapter)
It is fun and therapeutic for young children to play in water, but it is important that they have constant supervision. Never leave a

baby sitting alone in water for a second, regardless of how shallow the water or how well the baby can sit. It is too easy for a baby to slip and bump his head.

Let the children have fun on hot days by placing their paddling pool at the bottom of their slide. If the pool is very shallow, place some thick foam plastic in the pool as a landing pad!

On very hot days:
— place the paddling pool in shade. If there is none available, spread a tarpaulin or bedspread over the clothesline and place the pool under the shade of it;

— if the pool is not in the shade, have your children wear adequate protection against sunburn, such as hats, T-shirts and suntan lotion.

To keep paddling pools and swimming pools free of grass and other dirt on children's feet, put a large bowl of water beside the pool for them to step into before having their swim.

For a special treat, pour a little bubble bath in the paddling pool when you are filling it up. The children will find the bubbles lots of fun and they will be cleaning themselves in the process!

When the children have finished playing in the paddling pool for the day, give them old paint brushes, brooms, buckets and sponges to play 'house painter' and 'road workers'. You may find they are quite willing to paint (wash down!) parts of the house, patio or paths without realising they are helping.

Make sure you **empty the paddling pool** after using it each day.

PAINTING
Aprons

To help a child thoroughly enjoy himself while painting, **without having to worry about staining clothes,** give him an old plastic raincoat or an old, large shirt to wear back to front. Cut the sleeves back to size to prevent their dangling in the paint and knocking paint pots over.

Brushes and Alternatives

Make a paintbrush holder from a cardboard tube. Use the end of the tube as a stencil to cut around a piece of cardboard, to make a base for the container. Tape the base onto one end and use a rubber band around a piece of foil or plastic to keep the other end closed.

To keep paint brushes soft, get your children to clean them when they have finished with them and wrap them in plastic wrap before storing. (Make sure babies and small children do not use plastic wrap).

To protect the bristles of a fine paint brush, poke the end of it into a plastic drinking straw.

To make a small paint brush:
— keep the brushes from used empty bottles of nail polish. Use nail polish remover to clean them first;
— keep the small brushes that come with pots of paste and glue to clean and use as paint brushes;
— use old toothbrushes.

To give added variety to painting activities, try using some of the following objects with the paint, instead of brushes: feathers; sticks; leaves (dry and green); sponges (use pegs to hold the sponge); string; cotton buds; small pieces of carpet; small pieces of screwed up newspaper; discarded combs and brushes (hairbrushes, tooth brushes, bottle brushes, dishwashing brushes etc); plastic eye droppers (use food colouring or very thin paint).

Easels

To make it easier for young children to paint, place the paper on an easel. A simple improvisation of an easel is an old table tipped over on its side. Cover it with plastic or rubber sheeting and clip the paper on with bull-dog clips or spring pegs. Try to provide a box or table, beside the child at hip level, to stand the paints on.

Turn a blackboard into an easel for painting, by covering it with paper.

In fine weather:
— set up the painting activities outside. This will enable all concerned to be more relaxed about paint spillage and more able to enjoy the activity;
— use masking tape to stick the painting paper to the fence. Use a hose to wash the fence down at the end of the activity.

Encouraging Children To Paint

To encourage an unmotivated child to paint, work together with her. For instance, you could draw a snowman and some children playing and she could paint in the snow falling or you could draw the outline of a tree and she could cover it with leaves.

To keep young children's interest levels up when painting, introduce just one different activity and implement at a time. When you see the first signs of boredom, give them a different colour to use or a new object to paint with.

Finger Painting (see also Portrait Painting, this chapter)

To make paint suitable for finger painting, use one of the following recipes:

— stir a little water into 1/2 cup cornflour in a pot to make a paste. Add 300 ml boiling water and boil it until thick. Take it off the heat and mix in 1/2 cup soap flakes, some soap powder or a little detergent (this will make cleaning up afterwards easier). When it cools add dry powder paint;

— add dry powder paint to mixed wallpaper paste. The wallpaper paste can be mixed and kept in a plastic squeeze bottle. When it is required, squeeze just a small amount of paste into a container and add the colour. This should prevent too much wastage.

Use only two different colours to begin with. A young child will soon learn that when the two colours are mixed together they form a third colour. Blue and yellow will be good colours to start with as blue, yellow and green are some of the first colours children learn to recognise.

Marble Painting

To make a marble painting, place a piece of paper in a plastic bowl so that it comes up the sides a little. Using a plastic medicine dropper, drop several different coloured paints on to the paper. Place a marble in the bowl and tilt the bowl from side to side to allow the marble to take the paint around the paper and form interesting patterns. Closely supervise small children to ensure that the marble is not put into any mouths!

Paint Blowing

To give older children lots of fun, place just a dribble of thin paint on the paper and using a funnel, a straw or a cotton reel, let them blow it to form spider webs and other patterns. Remember there is a danger that younger children might suck up the paint instead of blowing it!

Paints

Keep paints in an old lunch box. When painting, the lid can be used to mix the colours while the base can be filled with water.

For an artist's palette, use: a plastic egg carton; an old patty tin, used for baking; an ice cube tray.

To prevent paint pots tipping over:
— stand the containers in a small milk bottle crate;

— cut holes in a large, thick piece of foam plastic for the pots of paint to sit in;

— sometimes packs of yoghurt etc come in plastic frames. Put the paint in the yoghurt pots when empty and put them back in the plastic frame to hold them together;

— pack the pots firmly in a shallow cardboard box or ice cream container (about 9 cm high) so that a slight knock with a hand or brush will not send them flying! Only give small quantities of each colour at a time, approximately 2 cm deep.

To make a water container for painting, which will not spill easily:
— punch a hole in the top of a screw-top jar, large enough to fit the brush in easily;

— use a heavy ashtray. With its flat base, it will not easily tip over and the cigarette grooves are great for resting the brushes on.

To keep the paint on the paper and to prevent it running too much:
— add one to two parts flour to two parts powder paint before mixing it with water;

— add liquid starch to the paint;

— experiment with some of the following thicker and rougher papers: several layers of newspaper; brown paper from a supermarket shopping bag; old wallpaper; blotting paper; coloured paper; several layers of computer paper.

If the paints in a paint box become hard, drop a little glycerine on each square. Leave the lid closed on the box for a few hours before using the paint.

To make a paint that will adhere to slippery surfaces, such as aluminium foil, plastic and glass, mix detergent powder, food colouring and egg yolk.

If you don't have any paint, mix up some food colouring with liquid starch.

Paper

Young children will find it easier to paint on thick, absorbent paper, such as thick brown paper, several layers of newspaper, blotting paper or cardboard.

When odd rolls of wallpaper are being sold cheaply, buy a roll or two to use as paper for your children to paint on. It is heavy enough to absorb large amounts of paint.

Portrait Painting

Children will enjoy painting their portraits, using a mirror:
— with finger paint, they can actually paint a picture of themselves on the mirror, which can be washed off afterwards;

— they can use the mirror to help them paint a picture of themselves on paper.

To get a child to paint a full picture of himself, lay him down on a large sheet of paper. Trace around his body with a crayon or pencil and he can paint his face, hair, clothes, fingers etc.

Preparing for Painting

To prevent plastic table cloths slipping off the painting table, dampen the table with a wet cloth before placing the plastic on top.

Use an old shower curtain as a table cloth when children are painting. It will only need to be wiped down at the end of the session.

If there is not a sink in the room, have a bucket of water and a cloth conveniently located for the children to wash their hands when necessary.

Printing

To make a stamp pad, cut the bottom off a fruit juice or milk carton, leaving the sides about 1 cm high. Cover the inside with a piece of hessian or sponge which has been cut to fit. Pour a little water-based paint under the sponge when ready to make the prints.

Use some of the following objects for printing: leaves (green and dry); hands; feet; pieces of cardboard; screwed-up paper; many types of vegetable and fruit (cut them in half, cut out the design of your choice on to the end of the vegetable and use these to make prints)

To make a scene when printing, consider some of the following ideas:
— make tree trunks from leeks or carrots cut vertically;

— make whole trees from pieces of broccoli or cauliflower cut vertically;

— make roads from celery;

— make clouds from the flower ends of broccoli or cauliflower or from a small balloon dipped in the paint;

— make wheels from the ends of carrots, leeks or cotton reels.

For a family activity, get a large sheet of paper and have everyone place their hand and foot prints on the paper. You may even be able to get your pets to make prints of their paws and feet too. Hang this on the wall.

Surprise Paintings

To paint a 'surprise picture', use a light-coloured crayon or wax candle to draw a picture on the paper. When the paper is covered with paint the picture which has been drawn, will show up.

Utilising Children's Paintings

To prevent paintings tearing:
— line the back edges and corners with masking tape;

— cover them with clear self-adhesive vinyl.

To display and store your child's paintings:
— put them in a photograph album under the plastic leaves;

— peg them on to wire coathangers and hang them from one or two hooks on the wall or ceiling;

— make a large collage to hang on the wall;

— paste them into a scrap book;

— hang them together on a skirt hanger. You can hang this from a hook on the wall and a different painting can be brought to the top for display each week;

— use the paintings as wrapping paper for presents;

— make them into a large book by punching holes on the sides of the paintings and either using a ring-binder clip or pieces of string to join them together. Stick ring-binder reinforcement stickers on the holes to prevent their tearing.

To make more permanent use of your child's paintings (remember to have the artist's name and date on the painting):
— stick them on to cardboard and make a jigsaw puzzle out of them;

— use them as cupboard and drawer liners. Place clear adhesive vinyl on the top so they can be wiped over with a damp cloth;

— get your child to write a letter to a friend or relative on the back of the painting, when it is dry.

PAPIER MACHE

To make papier mâché for children's models, make up a paste with one cup of flour mixed with cold water and bring it to the boil. Add boiling water until the paste is the right consistency, then add one teaspoon of alum to make the paste more adhesive. Grease the mould well with vaseline, tear the newspaper into strips about 2 cm by 15 cm, cover lavishly with paste and apply layer after layer to the mould until the desired thickness is reached, overlapping the edges well. Trim the edges and dry thoroughly before removing it from the mould. It can be dried in a warm oven. The model is then ready to paint.

PASTE

To make paste:
— blend 6 tablespoons cornflour with 1/2 cup cold water. Add 2 cups boiling water and boil for 1 minute until it becomes clear, then add 1/2 tablespoon disinfectant. If it is too thick, add a little more water;

— in a saucepan, mix one to two tablespoons of flour to a paste with a little water. Add another cup of water and mix it constantly while bringing it to the boil. Stir out all the lumps and allow to cool.

PLAY DOUGH

To make a very easy play dough, mix together 2 cups flour, 1 cup salt and enough water to make the right consistency. Add food colouring.

To make an extra smooth play dough, which lasts for ages, mix together in a saucepan 1 cup salt, 4 tablespoons cream of tartar and 2 cups plain flour. Add 2 cups water, food colouring and 2 tablespoons oil. Stir it well while cooking over a low heat for 3 - 5 minutes. As it is kneaded later, any lumps will disappear.

To store play dough, keep it in a covered, airtight container, such as a margarine container, preferably in the refrigerator.

When baking with pastry, keep the leftover pieces in plastic in the refrigerator for children to use as play dough. If you cook the model when it is finished the children will be really proud.

Keep play dough cutters, rolling pins etc in an old clear plastic flour canister.

PLAY MAT

To make a play mat that can be used to store toys, hem a large piece of brightly-coloured, durable fabric. Spread it on the floor for your child to play on and then gather up all the toys in it when they need to be put away and tie the corners into a knot to keep them together.

PLAYPENS *(see also* Camping *in* ON HOLIDAY *chapter)*

To prevent playpens being easily pushed around by energetic babies:
— make a floor for the playpen;

— tie a fabric playmat to the base of the playpen.

Wooden playpens can be used:
— to enclose a heater in winter. Ensure the heat is far enough away to prevent damage and fire;

— to enclose you when working on something which could be dangerous to children (such as a barbecue or sewing machine) or which could be endangered by children (such as a computer)!

To make a clothes' horse, from a wooden playpen, turn it up on its side. Hang the clothes over the rungs across the top and down the sides.

POLE TENNIS

To make a cheap version of pole tennis, place a table tennis ball (or some other light ball) into the toe of one side of an old pair of pantyhose. Tie a knot around the toe to secure the ball and nail the other end of the stocking into the top of a long piece of wood which has been driven into the ground. Use table tennis bats, or hands to hit the ball around.

POSTING

Small children enjoy playing 'postman'. Keep old envelopes in a box or bag for your children to sort and 'post'. Letter boxes can be made from old tissue boxes or cardboard boxes.

Cut different shaped holes in the tops of ice cream containers for your children to 'post' all sorts of things in. Stones can be posted into round holes, bus tickets into narrow slits, buttons into wider slits, bottle tops in another etc.

PUPPETS

To make finger puppets, use:
— little characters cut out from greeting cards. Make rings from thin strips of cardboard and attach these puppets to the rings;

— any blocks or toys which have holes that fit over children's fingers can become little imaginary 'people';

— small pieces of felt, sewn around the top to fit over the finger. Draw or sew on eyes.

To make 'sock puppets', use a crochet hook to pull wool through the weave of the sock for hair, sew on buttons for the eyes, pieces of felt for the nose and your hand will form the mouth between the fingers and thumb.

Paper plates make good puppets. Draw or paste on the face, ears, hair etc. Glue the plate to a cardboard tube to hold it by.

ROLLER SKATES

To remove dirt and grease from roller skate bearings, soak them in kerosene. Apply new grease before using them again.

SANDPITS

To make a sandpit:
— use a paddling pool that has a leak or is no longer required;

— buy an old tyre from a wrecker or a tyre shop. Fill it with sand and the children will be able to sit on the edge of the tyre to play;

— make a strong sand box with wood and nails. Make seats for the children to sit on by nailing a triangular piece of wood over each corner. Paint it a bright colour and put a set of castors on the bottom so that it can be rolled in or out of the sun;

— if you are going to use a tarpaulin or large sheet of heavy plastic to cover the sandpit, buy the tarpaulin first as they are usually sold in specific sizes. By doing this you will be able to make the sandpit so that the cover will fit correctly. Most of the covers have eyelets along the edges which can be used to hook over cup hooks which you can screw into the sides of the sandpit. Otherwise elastic loops can be sewn on to the sides to be hooked around the cup-hooks.

To make a cover for the sandpit:
— use a tarpaulin (as mentioned above);

— use a large sheet of hardboard;

— use a large sheet of plastic which you have folded around at the corners like a fitted sheet. Staple the corners so the cover can simply be lifted off and on.

To prevent too much rain gathering in puddles on the cover of the sandpit:
— place a piece of wood across the middle, from one side to the

other, before covering it with the tarpaulin. This will raise the cover in the middle, allowing the rain to run down and off the cover at the sides;

— place a bucket in the centre of the sandpit, under the cover, to act as a 'pie funnel'.

To keep children a little cleaner in the sandpit:
— always use washed river sand or fine silver sand in the box (builders sand often causes staining);

— make some cushions out of washable materials for the children to sit on while playing. The cushions will also prevent the children getting too cold if the sand is slightly damp.

To maintain a good standard of hygiene in the sandpit:
— don't allow children with diarrhoea or tummy upsets to play in the sand;

— keep animals off the sandpit by making sure that it is covered properly when it is not in use.

Teach your children never to throw sand. Make sure there is constant supervision if there is more than one small child in the sandpit at a time to prevent accidents with sand in eyes.

If sand does get into their eyes wash them out with plenty of cold water or place two or three drops of castor oil into the corner of the eye.

To prevent sand being carried into the house:
— have a clothes' brush at the back door, especially for the children to brush off the sand. Teach them how to do this properly before entering the house;

— place a bucket of water and an old towel near the sandpit each day so that the children can wash and dry their feet and hands before entering the house;

— keep the sandpit toys in a laundry basket in an outside shed or garage and encourage the children to shake the sand off all the toys carefully before putting them away.

To make a scoop for the sandpit, cut the bottom and half of one side off a plastic bottle, with a handle on it.

Some suggestions for toys to be used in the sandpit: rakes, combs, scoops, sieves, cups, watering cans, buckets of different sizes, shovels, plastic lids of all sizes from bottles and cans, jelly moulds, kitchen utensils, cookie cutters, toy cars, tractors, plastic flowers, shells, plastic animals etc.

Remember that children can have fun playing with wet sand as well as dry. They will be able to mould the sand into farms, towns, zoos, gardens etc.

SEWING

To help amuse your pre-schoolers while you try to sew:
— never throw away buttons! In fact become a collector and keep a jar of these colourful accessories by your sewing machine. Toddlers can thread the buttons with large holes, using a blunt bodkin, tied on to strong cotton and knotted at one end around a large button to form an 'anchor'. This will prevent it becoming lost. Keep the children with you while they are 'sewing';

— buttons can be sorted into different colours in a patty tin tray or an egg carton;

— pre-schoolers can learn to sew buttons onto material with an open weave that the bodkin will push through;

— buttons may be sorted by size in a line or pattern on the floor or on a tray.

To help a child thread a needle:
— stiffen the end of the thread by rubbing a little soap on it;

— spray some hairspray on your finger and then onto the end of the thread;

— hold a piece of white paper behind the eye of the needle, to make it easier to see the hole.

To teach a child how to use a sewing machine, let them practise on paper, without any thread in the machine. Draw roads on a large sheet of paper. Make some of the roads straight, some with curves, others with hairpin bends. Draw 'Stop' signs at T intersections and 'Slow' signs at bends, to remind them not to go too fast. When they get better at following the roads and the signs, let them try with thread in the machine and then on some fabric scraps.

SHAVING CREAM FUN

To give children a lot of tactile pleasure, let them play with shaving cream on a laminex or plastic table or bench top. They can make great designs and will just love the feel of it on their hands. It is also easy to clean up.

SHOPS

Children love to play 'shops'. Save little packets and containers for them to 'sell' in their shop. An old set of scales will be appreciated and a cash register or something that money can be kept in.

SKATEBOARDS
Before allowing a child to use a skateboard:
— have them taught how to fall properly (they should turn their head away from the ground as they fall and should try to roll as they hit the ground to spread out the impact of the fall);

— make sure they are wearing safety equipment, especially helmets;

— do not allow them to ride in traffic areas; .

— have them check their board each time for loose wheels or any other dangerous wear and tear.

SLIDES
If a slide is no longer slippery, rub some waxed paper over it.

SPEECH GAMES *(see also* **Word Games,** *this chapter)*
To develop skills of communication in young children:
— play 'What's in my bag?'. The child can use a hand bag or shopping bag or pillow slip to put something in from around the house. She then has to come to you and start describing it, without letting on what she has. Give her as long as possible to say all she can about the item before 'guessing' what it is that she has;

— cut out pictures from old magazines and stick them to pieces of cardboard. Pick out one picture at a time and ask your child to tell you a story about what is happening in the picture.

STILTS
To make a pair of simple 'stilts', use two empty tin cans of the same size and some strong string. On each tin, punch a hole on either side of one end. Thread through the holes a piece of string that is long enough for the child to hold on to while standing on the cans. He can walk around on the cans, like stilts, holding the strings in each hand.

SWIMMING *(see also* **Paddling Pools,** *this chapter)*
Babies and Toddlers
To help baby get used to swimming, introduce her to a shower when

she is young so she is not too troubled when water gets on her face.

When swimming with a baby or toddler, wear a T-shirt so he has something to easily grip on to for support.

Balls

To make a 'ball' for playing with in the pool, use the plastic insert from an empty wine cask. Wash them and fill them with air.

Swimming Safety

Wherever children are swimming:
— supervise young children at all times (children can drown in even five centimetres of water);
— do not be fooled into thinking that if your child has had swimming lessons he will be 'drown-proof'. It is a good idea to have your children taught to swim at an early age, but they must still be supervised at all times;
— do not allow children to chew anything while they are in the water, especially chewing-gum;
— do not allow children to dive into water before the depth has been checked;
— learn basic mouth-to-mouth resuscitation, especially methods used for young babies and toddlers.

Water In Ears

To keep water out of children's ears while they swim (bathing caps have to be tighter than most children can tolerate, to keep water out), mould some Blue Tac into the ear. This is especially good for children with grommets.

If your children have problems when they get water in their ears, keep a bottle of suitable ear drops (e.g. Swim Ear) with you at the pool or beach. The drops need to be administered straight away to be effective. Give them to your child's teacher to dispense, when your child has swimming lessons at school.

SWINGS

To stop the seat of a swing being too slippery, tack a rubber stair tread on to the wood. This will also prevent splinters and will dry quickly after rain.

Swings are great fun, but can be dangerous if:
— they are not securely fastened to the ground;

— they are placed over concrete. Place them on sand or bark or some other more 'forgiving' surface;

— they are not checked regularly for broken pieces and loose or missing bolts;

— young children are playing around them while others are playing on them. Make a rule that unless a child is using the equipment properly, he must stay well away, until it is his turn.

To soften the seat of a swing, cover it with foam plastic. Serious accidents have resulted from toddlers being hit by swings.

THREADING *(see Sewing, this chapter)*

To make a colourful necklace, wash and cut up several used plastic drinking straws into short pieces. Young children will be able to thread the short pieces with string and the longer pieces with a blunt bodkin.

To make colourful beads, dip pieces of macaroni, or other types of pasta that has holes in it, into different food colourings. When the macaroni is dry, thread the pieces on to nylon or cotton threads. Small children must be supervised as there is the danger that they may put the macaroni beads in their mouths and choke.

To make 'gold and silver' jewellery, thread pasta onto string or nylon thread and spray it with gold or silver paint.

To thread beads more easily:
— lay the beads, in order, down the grooves of a piece of corrugated cardboard;

— lay the beads on a piece of sticky tape, so each one stays put until required.

TOUCHING GAMES

To make a 'What am I Touching' game, fill a large, empty tissue box with lots of items of contrasting textures and shapes, such as a piece of playdough, a brush, a peg, a cotton wool ball, a feather, a stone, a table tennis ball, a piece of grass etc. The children have to close their eyes or reach up high and into the box, pull out an object and guess what it is. They can then set up the game for you.

TOYS *(see also Tidying in AT WORK chapter and IN THE BATHROOM)*
Boredom

To prevent children becoming bored with their toys:
— rearrange the toys by putting them in different places;

— divide the toys into two or three boxes. Give them just one box at a time and when they start to get bored with that lot, replace it with another box.

Buying Toys (see Toy Safety, this chapter)

When selecting toys for children of different ages, the following can be used as a general guide-line:

— **Under Six Months:** small washable soft toys, soft plastic blocks and balls, squeaky toys, rattles, mobiles, teething rings, pram beads, plastic books, 'activity centres', toys of different shapes and textures, toys which are sturdy, washable, unbreakable and with no sharp edges. They must be too big to swallow (no smaller than the child's clenched fist);

— **Six Months To One Year:** cuddly toys, push and pull toys, play mirrors, cardboard and cloth books, nests of blocks, containers to put things in, bath toys, simple musical instruments such as tambourines, bells and drums, sit-on toys, balls, activity centres;

— **One To Two Years:** cars, trucks, trains, building blocks, books, push and pull toys, toys for water play, crayons (non-toxic), telephone, 'ride-on' toys, play dough, bucket and spade and sand toys, puzzles, teddy bear, soft doll, threading activities, hammering toys, play animals, dressing up clothes;

— **Two To Three Years:** boats, books, tricycles, jigsaw puzzles, puppets, dolls, dolls' clothes, pram, dolls' house, broom, table and chairs, skittles, play dough, swings and slides, lawn mower, climbing frame, blackboards, records, paints (non-toxic), blunt scissors;

— **Four Years:** toy clocks, books, simple card games, dressing up outfits, hospital kit, play money, play shops, toy piano, modelling clay;

— **Five To Six Years:** board games, mouth organ, skipping rope, jigsaw puzzles, books, climbing frame, marbles, dominoes;

— **Seven Years and older:** sports equipment, kites, building tools, hobby and craft kits, roller skates, stamp and coin collections, sewing sets, model aeroplanes, bicycles etc.

Cleaning Toys

To clean plastic toys, rub with a damp cloth dipped in bicarbonate of soda. This should also take away any unpleasant odour.

Sharing Toys

To encourage your children to share swings, bikes and toys, use an egg-timer to give them turns of equal length. If the activities require longer turns, use the timer on the stove.

If a child wants to 'relieve' another child of a toy, make it a rule, that if Adam wants to 'share' what Jamie is playing with, Adam should have something to 'swap'.

To keep soft toys and dolls tidy:
— hang some fishing net from the ceiling to hold all the soft toys;

— keep the toys in a large hanging basket.

To clean soft toys:
— place them inside a pillowslip and tie it up before putting it in the washing machine and dryer. This will stop any fluff in the washing machine spoiling the toys;

— use carpet shampoo;

— place them in a nylon stocking to wash on a gentle cycle in the washing machine so they hold their shape. Hang them on the line with them still in the stocking to avoid peg marks;

— whisk up a solution of warm water and two tablespoons of detergent and scrub the toy gently with a nail brush. Rub it over with a clean cloth and then rinse it in warm water. Let it dry outside before brushing;

— put them in a bag containing cornflour. Shake the bag vigorously before brushing the toy thoroughly.

To give an old soft toy a new lease of life, knit a new set of clothes for it and sew the clothes firmly on top of the old material.

Storing Toys

To store children's toys, consider using some of the following:
— keep a basket or small toy box in each room that your children are likely to play in to make it easy to tidy up;

— stackable vegetable bins. They are light to carry, brightly coloured, easily cleaned and can be added to, stacked on top of each other to save space or divided up to place in different rooms;

— cardboard cartons, painted the same colour as the walls of the room in which they are kept;

— use large plastic ice cream containers with lids for small toys, such as sets of plastic zoo animals;

— small toys can be kept in a plastic hanging shoe rack;

— large toys can be kept in large plastic rubbish bins (make sure it is not taken outside on rubbish collection day!).

Toy Safety

To check on the safety of toys, use this guideline. The dangerous 'toys' are not usually the items purchased for children to play with, but rather the things which belong to adults and which children can reach and play with. Make sure that anything your baby can reach:

— is clean;

— has no sharp or pointed edges;

— is not light enough to be lifted, yet not heavy enough to cause damage if dropped;

— is not small enough to be choked on or swallowed (toys for a baby should be larger than the baby's fist and should not be able to fit into a 35 mm film container);

— cannot strangle;

— does not shoot or propel objects;

— is not poisonous, even if only licked or chewed;

— cannot suffocate;

— will not cause abnormal frustration and anger if broken!

Toys, such as skateboards, skates, bikes, trolleys and anything else with wheels are particularly dangerous when left lying around. Get your children to check the yard, before coming inside, and to put away all their toys.

TRAMPOLINES

Trampolines can cause nasty injuries if not used correctly. Children on a trampoline should be supervised at all times:

— do not allow more than one child to be jumping on a trampoline at a time;

— make sure there aren't any toddlers running around the trampoline while it is in use. Serious injuries can result from a toddler running underneath the trampoline while someone is jumping on it. Even if the person jumping is responsible, it is impossible to stop a jump half way through!

— if possible, have safety pads over the springs to prevent people jumping through them.

WATER PLAY
(see also **Coordination Games, Paddling Pools,** *this chapter)*

Playing with water can be very soothing, relaxing and therapeutic
for children. If you are having difficulty with your child's aggression
and hyperactivity, allow them to spend time playing with water. Let
them experiment with floating, pouring, sinking, splashing and
squirting, preferably outside. They can also bath their dolls, wash
their dolls' clothes and wash their tea-sets.

HASSLE-FREE LIVING WITH KIDS...
In the bathroom

(see also GROOMING)

BATHING BABY (see Slipping, this chapter)

Before bathing baby, take the telephone off the hook. Leave your watch beside it so you will remember to replace it afterwards.

Use muslin squares for washing baby. They are soft and fine enough to reach into baby's creases. They can be easily made by sewing two thicknesses of muslin together to make a square, approximately 18 cm by 18 cm. Use one coloured thread for the squares to be used on the bottom area and another coloured thread for the ones to be used on the face, to prevent infection.

To keep yourself dry while bathing baby, wear a plastic apron. Keep a towel between baby and the apron though, when carrying her, to stop her feeling too cold.

To check the temperature of baby's bath, feel it with the inside of your wrist.

To help settle a newborn baby who is unsure about having a bath, sing and talk to her and keep her feeling as secure as possible. She should feel more secure if her arms are kept down close to her body rather than up in the air.

It may be easier to bath a baby, if she is supported on a small, inflatable plastic ring.

To prevent a baby slipping in the bath:
— place a small towel, face washer, nappy or piece of foam plastic on the bottom of the bath;

— leave a soft singlet or T-shirt on the baby so your hands will be able to grip the infant better;

— wear a soft cotton glove on the hand that you hold him with;

— fill a hot-water bottle with warm water and sit the baby on it in the bathtub.

To save time, bath your baby with you in the big bath. Make sure there is someone handy to take the baby from you when her time is up. Preferably have that person dry and dress baby while you relax for a while longer in the bath!

To save your back from hurting too much when bathing a baby who has grown out of the small babies' bath, use the laundry tub. It is deep enough to contain the splashes and it saves you bending over the large bath. Make sure the tub has been thoroughly cleaned of course!

To help a baby feel secure on graduating to a big bath:
— sit the infant in a plastic clothes-basket. Being able to hold on to the sides will help him to feel safe. The water can flow in and out of the basket and the baby's bath toys can be kept handy;

— place the baby's bath in the big bath and bath baby in that until he is ready to venture out.

If your child is old enough to play without your holding her in the bath, but not old enough to be left alone, use the time to tidy the bathroom, sort through the cupboards, or clean the basins, toilets or walls. If you feel like sitting down instead, take the washing into the bathroom to fold or write out your next shopping list. From time to time your child would probably love you to play together with him.

Don't allow a baby to stand up in the bath by herself. She could easily fall and frighten or hurt herself.

To stop shampoo getting in baby's eyes, put a little petroleum jelly on the infant's eyebrows and eyelids. The water will run around it rather than over it.

To save having to lift a bath full of water:
— use a jug to empty it;

— use a short rubber shower hose to fill the bath. These can be bought fairly cheaply and are normally used for washing hair in or over the bath. Preferably place the baby's bath on the vanity next to the basin and fill it up. To empty it, place the end of the hose in the bath, run a little more water through it, from the taps so that the hose fills up and then take the hose off the taps and let the water drain into the basin.

Drying Baby

To make baby more comfortable, place a thin sheet of foam plastic underneath the bath towel on the change table. This will absorb the dampness and prevent slipping.

In winter, keep a baby warm after a bath by warming a large beach towel to wrap around her. It will help her to feel secure and snug. Warm clothes will also make her feel good. Warm them in front of a fire, a heater or in the clothes' dryer for a few minutes.

To prevent a baby being startled by cold baby lotion, place the bottle of lotion, tightly closed, in hot water or in the bath tub while you are bathing him. It will be warm enough to apply when needed. Warm shampoo in this way too.

BATH TOYS

To keep a child's bath toys out of the way:
— store them in a nylon- or plastic-mesh bag. Tie some string on to a plastic clothes peg, which you can use to secure the top of the bag, and hang the string round one of the taps.

— keep them in a bicycle basket hung from the shower rail;

— keep them in a string shopping bag, hung over the taps.

To help make bath time a lot of fun:
— make a simple hand puppet from a face washer or an old piece of towelling. It can be used as a wash cloth too.

— let them experiment with floating, pouring, sinking (not themselves!), splashing and squirting (within the confines of the bath tub!), using kitchen utensils, for example: ice cube trays, plastic bottles, measuring spoons, colanders, pastry brushes, egg cups, funnels, tea strainers and small watering cans (not all at once!).

— allow an older child to play with some of his beach toys.

To sanitise bath toys, soak them regularly in a nappy sterilising solution. Any toys which fill up with water and don't drain completely between baths should not be used.

CHILDREN IN THE BATH

(see **Slipping** *and* **Soap,** *this chapter and* **IN FAMILIES** *chapter)*

To entice your children into the bath: tell them that the last one in will have to clean the bath.

Encourage young children to wash themselves by giving them their own special sponge and soap.

To coax your children from the bath when they don't want to get out, pull out the plug! It is not a good idea to pull the plug out while a baby is in the bath as the noise could frighten her. Seeing the water rush down the plug hole could also be frightening. Even when the plug has been pulled out, don't leave a toddler or baby in the bath as accidents have happened when children have replaced the plug or when an object has blocked the plug hole and the taps have been turned on.

Some children detest having baths. If your child appears fearful of water and having a bath, consider some of the following procedures:
— cover the bath plug with a bath mat or towel;

— never let the plug out while your child is in the bath, unless they want you to. Some children are afraid of the noise and think they may be sucked down too. If your bath makes a particularly loud noise as it is emptying, keep a short length of hose in the bathroom. When you take the plug out, quickly stand one end of the hose on the drain hole and hold the other end above the water level. The hose will release the air that is trapped in the pipe beneath the plug, which causes the noise;

— try to keep as calm as possible at bath time and just give a quick, gentle bath before wrapping her up securely in a large towel and giving her a big cuddle;

— if your child is really terrified, stop bathing her altogether for a period of time and just give her sponges with a bowl of water;

— when the weather is warm, play with the hose and water outside so she gets used to getting water on her face.

CHILDREN IN THE BATHROOM
(see Dangerous Objects and Substances, following)

To remind children to use the same towels, toothbrushes, face washers etc, give each child one colour for all the items.

If the towel rail is too high for a child to reach his towel, lap just a few centimetres of the end of the towel over the rail and use clip pegs or safety pins to hold it on.

To make it easier for children to pull out plugs in the hand basin, place a key ring around the loop in the plug.

DANGEROUS OBJECTS AND SUBSTANCES

Remember that if your toddler sees daddy shaving his whiskers and splashing after-shave over his face, or mummy shaving her legs and putting mascara on her eyelashes, he will be keen to have a go. If you have a particularly inquisitive child who likes to copy everything you do, be very selective about what you allow him to watch you doing. Make a conscious effort at all times to keep the following bathroom items out of reach of children. That will mean putting them away out of reach immediately after you have used them:

— razors and razor blades; after-shave lotions and shaving creams; cosmetics, perfumes and nail polish; bubble bath, shampoos and conditioners; scissors;

— medicines;

— cleaning agents, disinfectants and bleaches;

— toilet fresheners (the substance paradichlorbenzene, which is found in moth balls and in toilet fresheners, which are wrapped in pretty bright paper, is very dangerous and can cause breathing difficulties. A child left alone in the toilet could find them very inviting!);

— everything in glass containers.

Never leave small children unsupervised in the bathroom. Keep bathroom and toilet doors securely closed when not in use if there are children in the house. Young children can drown in the small amount of water in the toilet and there are too many potential dangers in the bathroom.

Dispose of used razor blades in a money box or soft drink can on a high shelf and keep new razor blades well out of reach of children.

Don't keep any potentially dangerous items in cabinets above the toilet or above the bath as a child could climb on these to reach what he is looking for.

ELECTRICITY

Never use a portable electric heater in the bathroom.

Don't leave any electrical appliances, such as hair dryers, hair tongs and shavers near a source of water and teach your children as early as possible to make sure their hands are completely dry before touching anything electrical.

HAIR-WASHING *(see* GROOMING *chapter)*

HOT-WATER

To help children easily identify hot-water taps, mark them clearly with red tape and teach small children that red means danger! (You can use red tape to identify other dangerous items around the home.)

If the hot-water tap drips over the bath, tie a towel around the tap to save accidents, while waiting to get it fixed. (Don't delay in getting it fixed!)

To avoid burns in the bathroom:
— always run the cold water into the bath first and turn the hot tap off first. If you have a mixer tap, run a little cold water through the taps before turning it off and leave it on the cold setting in case some water drips or the child manages to turn it on;

— keep your hot water temperatures down to between 50°C and 55°C while you have children in the house. Water at the temperature of 66°C will produce a third degree burn in two seconds!

— wrap a towel around the hot tap if it is still hot when your children get into the bath.

LOCKS

To prevent small children locking themselves in the bathroom:
— cover the top of the door with a towel, which will prevent it closing properly;

— make sure locks inside bathrooms are too high for a child to operate;

— install locks on bathroom and toilet doors that can be opened from the outside in an emergency.

PLANNING A NEW BATHROOM

Plan to have the basin placed more to one side of the vanity. This will allow extra bench space on the other side for towels, children while washing their feet, baby while changing his nappy, the baby bath and so on.

Place the bathroom cupboard door handles higher than normal and install child-proof locks on cupboards that store dangerous objects.

Remember, **when choosing bathroom tiles,** that glossy tiles on the floor will become very slippery and dangerous when wet.

SLIPPING

To prevent slipping in the bathroom:
— lay non-skid mats on the bottom of the bath and on the floor of the shower;

— lay a towel on the bottom of the bath;

— install a handle on the wall, by the bath, to grab onto in case of a fall;

— use bath mats and teach your family to wipe up any water or liquid spills as soon as they occur. This is especially important if you have shiny tiles on the floor.

TEETH CLEANING *(see* GROOMING *chapter)*

TOILETS *(see also* Toilet Training *in* DEVELOPMENT *chapter)*

To help young children become independent in the bathroom, keep a light-weight stool handy for them to carry to the basin or toilet when they need extra height.

To prevent children pulling all the paper off the toilet roll, squeeze the roll together to flatten it a little before inserting it on to the holder.

Remember that most young children have a fascination with water. A favourite past-time for many children is to throw things into the toilet and some like to retrieve them as well! It is possible for a child to drown in a toilet! Always keep toilet and bathroom doors shut when you have a toddler around and keep the toilet seat down. Keeping the toilet flushed and regularly cleaned could reduce some hygiene problems if a child did manage to investigate the area.

If there are windows in the bathroom behind the toilet or above the bath, have them 'child-proofed' to prevent any 'exploring climbers' falling out! Fit safety catches or locks which children cannot undo.

WARNING: Never mix household bleach with other cleaning products. The gas created is very dangerous. Neither should you mix different types of toilet cleaners.

HASSLE-FREE LIVING WITH KIDS...
In the bedroom

(see also IN TRANSIT)

BABIES IN BED
Bassinets

To prevent a newborn baby rolling on to his back, from his side while sleeping, place a soft toy or a rolled up towel behind his shoulders.

To keep the bassinet mattress covered securely:
— put it inside a pillowcase instead of using a bottom sheet;

— make buttonholes in each corner of the sheet and then sew a button on each corner of the mattress to button the sheet on with. This will prevent the sheet crumpling up under baby's back while asleep.

Bumper Pad

Bassinet mattresses can be used as a bumper pad for a cot. Put a decorated pillow slip over it, which can be removed for washing.

Carrycots

To eliminate any possibility of baby rolling out of a carrycot, when you are changing it from one hand to the other, tie the handles together.

Sleeping Babies

To show that baby is sleeping, hang a picture of a sleeping infant on the nursery door. Siblings and visitors will know to be quiet when they see it.

Bedding (*see also* Cots, *this chapter*)

Blankets

When storing blankets off the children's beds in summer, fold them up and place them in an old pillowslip. They will stack more neatly and not collect dust.

To repair old, torn blankets, cut out the shapes of animals from stuffed toy patterns and applique them on to the worn areas. Embroider eyes, mouth, nose, etc., on to the animal shape. If you don't have any patterns, trace some from children's colouring books.

Duvets and Doonas (*see* Quilts, *following*)

Mattresses

To protect the mattress on a young child's bed, use an old shower curtain.

Quilts

To protect an expensive or light-coloured quilt or duvet when children are playing in their rooms, cover it, through the day, with a fitted sheet over the bed.

To stop a quilt sliding off the bed, find a piece of sheeting as close to the colour of the quilt cover as possible and sew it to the bottom end of the cover, to be tucked in under the mattress.

To make an inexpensive doona or duvet cover for a single bed, buy two sheets and join them together. Stitch them around three sides and put large press studs or a zip on the remaining side. If you need curtains for the room, buy extra matching sheets to make into curtains. Plain sheets can be made into decorative doona covers if you applique different shapes on to the fabric.

Use an old continental quilt as an under-blanket. Turn it around so the flaps tuck in at the top end, to prevent it wrinkling underneath the sheet. It will be easily washed and can be made even more firm by sewing two pieces of elastic from the flap on one side to the flap on the other, to hold it underneath the mattress.

Use an unzipped sleeping bag as a quilt on a child's bed in winter. To stop it sliding off the bed:
— tuck a sheet or blanket on top of it;
— lay it lengthwise across the bed to allow for extra tuck-in at the sides.

Sheets (see Bassinets, this chapter)

To make a fitted sheet, tie a knot in each corner of a normal sheet and tuck in under the mattress.

If your child is a restless sleeper and messes up the bed a lot, lay the sheets lengthwise across the bed so that there is more to tuck in on the side.

If you don't have a valance for your child's bed, place a fitted sheet over the bed base. It will look attractive when coordinated with the duvet or doona.

BEDROOMS

Bed-making (see AT WORK chapter)

Beds

Headboards on beds can be potentially dangerous to young children. Young babies have been known to get their heads stuck in the gap between the headboard and the mattress. Make sure this cannot happen on your children's beds.

For a 'spare bed', cover an old, light single mattress with a plastic cover and keep it under your child's bed. It will easily slide in and out and can be used as a gymnastic mat when your children are feeling energetic.

Bedside Tables

If you don't have bedside tables for your children, cover a wooden box or strong cardboard carton with plastic contact to match the decor. It will help your children keep their belongings in order and will be easy to keep clean.

Change Tables (see Nappies in AND THEIR CLOTHES chapter)

Clothes' Drawers

To keep your children's clothes' drawers tidy and in order:
— place chocolate boxes, shoe boxes and ice cream containers in the drawers to create separate areas for socks, singlets, pants, tights, hankies and so on. Name each one or stick a picture of the article on the outside;
— label each drawer so the children are reminded what belongs inside. Pictures of the appropriate garments can be pasted on to the front of the drawers with the corresponding words written alongside.

Cots

To stop blankets being kicked off in the night:
— sew loops of elastic on to the corners of the blankets. Either tie them in a bow to the rails of the cot or use press studs to hold them on. The elastic will allow the child to move around a little without the blankets coming off;
— place a pair of men's braces under the mattress or cot and clip them to each side of the blanket or cover.

To stop a toddler rocking the cot from one side of the room to the other, place pieces of sponge rubber under each leg of the cot.

To keep your baby amused in bed, hang a large soft ball from a ceiling hook over the cot so that he can pat or kick it. Remove this when baby becomes old enough to stand up, to prevent accidents happening with the cord.

If you want to keep baby's hands away from the walls in his bedroom, place his cot diagonally out from the corner of his room. It will be difficult for him to reach the walls and easy for you to change the sheets.

Curtains

To stop light leaking through the gap between the curtains, sew pieces of velcro along the edges and stick them together.

If you have net curtains, but no fly screens in the children's bedrooms, run a curtain wire along the bottom as well as the top of the net curtains hanging on the windows. Attaching the wire to the lower window sill will keep out a lot of insects.

To make original and inexpensive curtains for your children's rooms, buy plain-coloured fabric and applique some brightly-coloured shapes, designs or pictures of animals etc.

If your baby insists on pulling and playing with long curtains, tuck the curtains through a coat hanger and hook it over the curtain rod, out of baby's reach while he is around. Hang them up this way too while washing inside windows to keep the curtains out of the way.

Decorating Children's Rooms

To brighten up a blank wall in a child's room:
— mount a large piece of cardboard on the wall and display photographs of family, friends and pets;

— use self-adhesive vinyl to cover pictures of interest to your children, from old calendars and magazines. They can then be hung on the wall as posters;

— hang a mirror securely to the wall. Not only should the mirror help with their grooming, but young children can keep themselves amused for ages, just looking at themselves.

Make attractive notice boards for your children's rooms by covering large pieces of polystyrene or cork with fabric, to match the decor of the room. Pictures, photographs, posters, library cards and reminder notices can all be pinned up without damaging the walls.

To make a frieze for your child's room:
— cut the pictures from an old calendar, join them side by side with tape on the back and hang it around the wall. Check to see if the pictures on this year's calendars are suitable to use before discarding them;

— have several photographs enlarged to join together to make a frieze. Photographs of different members of the family, friends and pets will be especially popular. If it is too expensive to have the enlargements done, stick the regular photographs on to larger pieces of different coloured card. Join those together and hang it around the wall, low enough to be easily seen.

Lights and Lamps

To make it easier to check on your children while they sleep and to feed babies at night without waking them up too much:
— install a dimmer switch in their bedroom. They are not too expensive and are easily installed;

— replace the normal light bulb with a blue bulb.

To prevent bedside lamps being knocked over:
— glue the lamp to the centre of a fairly large wall or floor tile. It will look good if the tile coordinates with the decor.

— tape the power cord to the legs of the table.

Mobiles *(see also* **AT PLAY** *chapter)*

To hang light mobiles:
— attach a plastic hook with adhesive backing to the ceiling;

— after using a drawing pin to hang the thread on the ceiling, cover the pin with blue tack to hold it more securely.

Don't hang any mobiles directly above baby's cot unless you are sure that it could not fall into the cot. The ornaments and strings attached could be dangerous for a baby to play with.

When buying mobiles:
— check that they hang at the right angle to be seen properly from the baby's vantage point, not necessarily yours;

— check that they would not be dangerous if they fell within reach of baby.

When your children have finished with their mobiles, use the figures from them to decorate the Christmas tree.

Storage

To hang coats, bags etc in a child's bedroom, hang a row of 'cloakroom hooks' on the wall at the appropriate height. You can buy them in many different colours to coordinate with the room.

Wardrobes

To make it easier for small children to reach their clothes, place an extension rod at their level in the wardrobe. Hang two cords of equal length down from the original rod. Make a loop at each end and slide another rod through the two loops to hold it in place. If it is a double wardrobe you may decide to make a more permanent lower rail on one side, which can be used later for hanging skirts and blouses.

Waterbeds

Waterbeds are very dangerous for small babies. The mattress moulds around the baby and could prevent him being able to breathe. Don't leave babies on waterbeds!

CHILDREN IN BEDS
Changing From Cot to Bed

To encourage a toddler to change over from a cot to a bed:
— start the child off sleeping on the mattress on the floor, so that he knows he won't hurt himself if he falls out of bed;

— place the child in the bed next to the wall and the cot next to the bed so the nearby bars of the cot maintain a secure feeling. Gradually move the cot further and further away from the bed;

— attach safety rails to the sides of the bed and if he is feeling insecure, explain that these will prevent him falling out;

— tuck the top sheet lengthwise across the bed so there is a good tuck-in on each side, making it less likely for a child to fall out;

— lay the cot mattress, or some other 'landing pad' on the floor next to the bed, so that the child will know he won't hurt himself if he does happen to fall out!

Day-Time Naps

To get your baby used to sleeping in different places, so she will settle better when you take her out:

— if you have a portable cot, put her down to sleep in it in different parts of the house during the day, so she doesn't get too dependent on one particular place for sleeping;

— make up little beds for her in different parts of the house during the day and don't try too hard to keep everything quiet around her. If she gets used to sleeping in silence, she may not be able to sleep in places that are not as quiet.

To encourage a reluctant child to take day time naps:

— provide a hum of background noise, e.g. a vacuum cleaner turned on outside the room, a fan turned on in the room, some gentle music, a washing machine turned on nearby, an untuned radio turned on etc.

— make a comfortable little hut or nook in a corner, surrounded by chairs or under a large table;

— make a 'nest' in a huge, well-ventilated, padded cardboard box. If this is successful you could help your little one to decorate it with pictures and drawings to be used more often;

— if your child has a sleeping bag, let her use it in winter to nap, perhaps on your big bed or somewhere new.

If your child no longer needs to sleep, set aside time each day for rest and quietness. Perhaps you can think up a special name for this time. Provide some books and soft toys to play with on the bed.

To stop your child calling out every few minutes during his rest time to ask 'is time up?':

— have a clock in his room and show him where the hands need to be before he can get up. Perhaps put a toy clock beside it with the hands at the right time so he can tell when they are the same;

— play several records or set a timer to play tapes of gentle music for as long as the rest time is to be. Tell him he can get up when the music has completely finished;

— let your child know that you will call him and that he is not to call you. To assure him that you will not forget, let him see you set a timer.

Early Wakers

To encourage an early waker to amuse herself quietly in the mornings when she first wakes up, while you attempt to sleep a little longer:
— place some safe toys and books where she can reach them in the morning;

— leave a safe activity on a small table for your child to do when she wakes up. Lay it out on the table after she has gone to sleep so that she won't be tempted to play with it when she is supposed to be going to sleep and so it is a surprise for her in the morning. Choose such things as puzzles, blocks, colouring-in, drawing paper and pencils, books to read, play dough, shapes to trace around etc. If your child hasn't learnt how to keep things clean around her you will need to choose carefully or you may have a redecorating job on your hands!

To show your children when they are allowed to come into your room in the mornings, have a toy clock in their room with the hands pointing to the time you set. Have a real clock next to it and tell them that when the real clock is the same as the toy clock they may knock on your door.

Getting Children Into Bed

To keep children feeling happy and secure at bed time, it is a good idea to develop a few routines, e.g. try to stick to the same bed time each night, quieten the children down with a bath, a story and a drink, clean their teeth, sit up in bed to sing a few songs, talk about the day, say prayers and lights out.

To prepare your children for going to bed:
— tell them that they 'only have ten more minutes to play before it is bed time' — and then stick to it! It is much better to give them plenty of warning than to suddenly break the news to them that they must abandon what they are doing immediately. This is a good habit to get into when getting children to stop playing, to come for meals and so on;

— discourage them from starting a new game just before bed time. It will be difficult to get their cooperation if they have just become excited about their new activity or game.

To encourage young children to go with you upstairs to bed (sometimes they can be too heavy to carry, but too tired to climb the stairs without encouragement):

— hang a piece of clothing as a 'tail' out of his pyjamas and tell him you are chasing his tail;

— give them a 'ticket' to go upstairs. Children love tickets;

— make up a game incorporating their latest story-book heroes to get them up the stairs, e.g. you can be the gingerbread man, singing 'run, run as fast as you can, you can't catch me, I'm the gingerbread man', all the way up to their rooms. (Singing while going up the stairs is much less exhausting than carrying a heavy toddler!)

Bed time for children is important and should be kept as peaceful and as cosy as possible. Avoid using bed time as a punishment!

To make bed time a special time:

— use this time for lots of cuddles and to whisper secrets in your child's ear;

— tell your children that before you say 'Goodnight' and leave the room you are going to give them three butterfly kisses (you blink your eyelashes against the child's eyelashes), one caterpillar kiss (you kiss his arm with fast little kisses from his fingertips to his shoulder), four pig kisses (you make pig noises while you kiss him around the neck and chin) and one bear hug (you give him a great big hug).

Getting Out of Bed

If your child frequently gets out of bed for drinks, leave a plastic bottle, containing water, next to the bed so she does not need to leave the room. A drink bottle which comes fitted with its own plastic straw through the lid is ideal as it reduces the chance of water being spilt by unsteady hands in the dark. You will probably find that not as much water is required after all.

Wet Beds

To save time changing beds in the night:

— make up the baby's cot with two sets of sheets and waterproof sheeting underneath each other. When the sheets need changing in the night, simply remove the top set. The top sheet need only be a half sheet;

— use 'sheet bags' made from single sheets, by folding them in half and sewing along the end and down one side. If small children are sleeping in big beds or sleeping bags, this will also stop them moving around too much and getting lost in the bed or bag.

To remove stains after bed-wetting accidents, sprinkle talcum powder over the area, leave it for a few hours and then brush or vacuum it off. ▬

If the bed still feels damp after removing the wet bedding, use a hair dryer to dry out any damp spots on the mattress.

COLD WEATHER *(see also* **Bedding,** *this chapter and* **Pyjamas** *in* **AND THEIR CLOTHES** *chapter)*

To help settle an infant in winter, warm the bed with a hot-water bottle before putting the baby in it. This will be especially helpful after night feeds. Put the hot-water bottle in the bassinet while you are feeding, but be sure to remove it before putting baby back to bed.

To make a simple hot-water bottle cover for an older child's bed, sew together two face cloths, leaving an opening at the bottom for the tag. Tape can be used at the top to tie it together. Note: Never put a baby in bed with a hot-water bottle, just use it to warm up the bed first. With an older child, always face the hot-water bottle down towards the bottom of the bed in case it does happen to leak.

To increase the humidity in a child's room in winter, hang some wet towels on a play pen, changing table or clothes' horse in front of a heater (make sure the heater is recommended for use in a child's room).

HOT WEATHER

To keep a baby cool in summer, beach towels can be used instead of blankets. They are not as hot as blankets and can easily be washed and dried.

To help cool down a child when it is very hot, fill a hot-water bottle with cold or iced water and put it in the bed.

SICK CHILDREN IN BED
Amusing Children in Bed *(see also* **AT PLAY** *chapter)*

Give the children a tray, with sides on, to use for the following activities: play dough and modelling clay; playing cards; puzzles; colouring-in; miniature dolls house; miniature racing track.
This will prevent the child becoming frustrated with things sliding

everywhere and will make it easier to tidy up afterwards.

If a child will be in bed for a long time, consider setting up some of the following:
— a portable cassette player. Teach him how to use it to play music and stories. You could read some stories on to a tape for your child to read along to. Remember to give a signal on the tape, to non-readers, to tell them when to turn the page;

— a goldfish in a bowl, bird in a cage or a white mouse in a cage. The child will enjoy being able to look after them and talk to them;

— get him to plant some fast-growing seeds which he can watch growing;

— perhaps a television set could be set up and encourage other members of the family to watch it with the sick child.

To encourage children to draw and colour-in while they are sick, give them a new set of crayons or coloured pencils.

When your child is sick in bed, try to spend as much time with him in his room as possible:
— take ironing, mending, washing to fold etc into the room with you so that you can chat or just be there while you work;

— use this time to spring clean the child's room, so long as you don't lift dust or create fumes from cleaning agents.

Comforting Children in Bed

To make a child more comfortable, while sick:
— make the bed regularly, to keep the sheets as smooth as possible;

— make a table to go over their legs by inverting a cardboard box and cutting an arch out of both sides.

Make a handy bedside table for children to put all their books and play things on when sick in bed, by adjusting the ironing board to the correct height and covering it with a protective cloth.

To make it easier for a child to put on a cardigan in bed, get them to put it on back-to-front, with the buttons down the back. With her back leaning against pillows she may not need to have them done up, but it will be easy to slip on and off.

Food and Drinks in Bed (see also Reluctant and Slow Eaters in AT MEAL TIMES chapter)

To help eliminate spills, when giving children drinks in bed:

— use a plastic bottle or cup that comes with a straw through its lid;

— keep the plastic cup and its fitting lid, with a hole in it for a straw, that drinks are served in at some fast food chains.

— punch a hole in the lid of a screw-top jar. Fill the jar with the drink, screw on the lid and poke a straw through the hole;

— save a baby's trainer cup, with a lid, to use when children are sick.

To protect the mattress from any spills and accidents, while a child is sick, tuck a large beach towel into the mattress around where the child will be sitting.

HASSLE-FREE LIVING WITH KIDS...

And their clothes

APRONS

To make it easier for children to tie their own aprons:
— make the ties twice their normal length, when sewing them, so they can be brought around to the front for tying;

— make the ties wide. Narrow strings tend to tangle.

Make a 'poncho' to cover your children's clothing, **to keep them clean when they are ready to go out.**

BABY CLOTHES

Keep small items of baby clothing together in ice cream containers, e.g. booties, socks, shoes, bibs, bonnets etc.

To stop white baby clothes turning yellow:
— wash them first and rinse in a solution of 1 teaspoon vinegar

to 1 litre water, before drying and storing them between layers of blue tissue paper;

— fold the gowns with tissue paper between the material and in the folds. Then wrap in blue paper to prevent yellowing. Finally, wrap in several sheets of newspaper before packing into a cardboard box with a good sprinkling of epsom salts in the bottom. The printers' ink and epsom salts will discourage moths and silverfish.

When baby has grown out of the smallest sized clothes, choose some suitable ones to be kept for your daughter's dolls' clothes collection. A doll can be very expensive to dress.

BELTS

To help small children buckle up their own belts, paint a dot next to the hole they are to use.

To make an inexpensive belt, sew a clip buckle on to the end of a piece of wide, black elastic. White elastic can be dyed to the appropriate colour as well.

Belt loops from trousers and skirts can be used in children's cardigans and coats. Cut them off the trousers before discarding and sew them inside the necklines of clothes that need to be hung up on a hook.

BIBS (see also **AT MEAL TIMES** chapter)

To make a special bib for best, make it out of scraps of the fabric used to make the dress or top. It will be inconspicuous, and can be made to look decorative with a little bit of lace or binding.

If you don't have a clean bib handy, use safety pins to pin a face cloth to the child's clothes.

To keep a teething ring, light rattle or dummy handy, tie a ribbon around it. Sew a press stud or dome to the other end of the ribbon and one on to the bib. Attach the teething ring on to the bib so it won't drop on the floor and get dirty. Make sure the ribbon is not long enough to wrap around baby's neck.

To recycle towelling bibs when your children have grown out of them, cut off the ties and use as face cloths.

BOOTIES

To keep booties together:
— use small, plastic curtain hooks;

— use a knitting stitch holder to pin several pairs of booties together at once;

— clip them together with pegs and keep them all in a box or ice cream container so they won't become scattered around the drawer.

To save losing the ties and ribbons on booties, sew them to the back seams when you are making the booties so they can't pull out.

When washing booties:
— peg them together on a coathanger and then peg the hanger on the clothes' line. This will save them getting tangled up in the rest of the washing and will save you hunting for them later;

— keep the pairs together with a safety pin to save them getting misplaced in the washing machine and on the line.

BOWS *(see also* **Hair Accessories** *in* **GROOMING** *chapter)*

To get a bow on a dress to sit properly, cross it from left to right first and then use the left hand side again to make the first loop.

If the necklines of any garments are too tight, remove the buttons and replace with bows which can be done up more loosely.

BUTTONS *(see also* **Sewing Children's Clothes,** *this chapter)*

To lengthen the life of buttons on children's clothes, sew them on with shirring elastic instead of cotton. This should withstand the tugging of little fingers better and will make it easier for children to do up their own buttons.

When teaching a toddler to do up buttons:
— start with large buttons;

— get her to start doing them up from the bottom of the garment, where she can see them more easily.

Button on babies' clothing are potentially dangerous. When you buy clothes, check to see that the buttons are sewn on securely. If in doubt, reinforce them. Babies love to put buttons in their mouths and they could easily inhale or choke on them.

CARDIGANS *(see* **Woollens,** *this chapter)*

COLD WEATHER

To determine whether a baby is cold or not, feel his chest, back and abdomen rather than just his feet and hands. If his skin feels cool, he probably needs something warmer on, if he feels damp, he is probably too hot and if he is warm, just right.

If your baby is cold:
— hold him close or put him in the sun or a warm room to warm him up before putting on more clothes;

— dress him in two thinner layers rather than one thick layer as the air held between the layers will act as insulation;

— wool and cotton are much warmer than man-made fabrics.

CRAWLERS
(see **Overalls, Crawlers** and **Pyjamas** and **Long Pants** this chapter)

DRESSES (see also **Hems** and **Storage,** this chapter)
To lengthen a little girl's dress:
— use ribbon, braid or lace to cover the change in fabric colour;

— add a ruffle, made from coordinating fabric, around the bottom of the dress.

To get maximum wear from little girls' sun-frocks, invest in a little white blouse for her to wear underneath the dress when the weather becomes a little cooler. Different coloured T-shirts can be worn underneath as well, to give the appearance of a well-coordinated outfit.

To protect special little dresses while storing, cover them with old pillow-slips. Cut a small hole in the centre of the closed end of the pillow-slip to poke the coat hanger hook through and pull the slip down over the dress. Flower-girl dresses should keep well this way.

Take the creases out of a velvet dress by hanging it on a coathanger in the bathroom while someone is having a hot shower. Keep the door closed and the steam will straighten it out.

DRESSING BABIES AND TODDLERS (see also **Shoes,** this chapter)
When dressing newborn babies, remember that they can feel very insecure without clothes on. They don't seem to appreciate the feeling of air on their bodies and their arms exposed, so keep the time of their 'exposure' to a minimum and where possible hold their little arms down close to their bodies with one hand while working with the other.

To help distract a restless toddler you are trying to dress:
— sing a favourite song and encourage him to sing along;

— give him a small object to play with while dealing with his bottom half! He should particularly enjoy small containers with lids which open and shut;

— make a game of 'peek-a-boo' with the arms and legs you are putting in and pulling out of garments;

— hold your baby still, standing between your legs, while you pull up long pants and tights.

DRESSING IN THE MORNINGS

To save time in the mornings:
— select the children's clothes the night before for the following day and lay them out ready to put on. Include everything from socks to cardigan. That way you can discover any problems with clothes when you still have time to do something about it;

— leave the children's clothes, for the following day, hanging up on a rail that they can reach themselves (*see* Wardrobes *in* AT BEDTIME *chapter*) or on a hook behind the door;

— if the children are allowed to choose which clothes they will wear, get them to do that the night before and if you have a child who likes to model several combinations of clothing before deciding on the set to wear, make a rule that once they have chosen their clothes they are not allowed to change their minds (unless you are happy for a lot of time to be spent dressing in the mornings).

GLOVES AND MITTENS (*see also* **Booties,** *this chapter*)

To prevent a child losing her gloves or mittens:
— sew the mittens to each end of a piece of ribbon or tape, long enough to be threaded up through the sleeves and across the inside of the back of the coat or jacket. When they need to be taken off to use the hands they won't be able to be dropped;

— sew an elastic loop to the top of each glove or mitten and either loop these to buttons on the children's cuffs or safety pin them to the insides of their cuffs.

HAND-ME-DOWNS

To give a special, personalised touch to children's hand-me-down clothes:
— choose a favourite animal or toy to applique on to the garment. You can buy them quite inexpensively and they make useful cover-ups for stains and worn areas;

— dye the garment;

— sew on some lace trim, a bow or some colourful buttons.

When storing clothes in readiness for your next child:
— place them in boxes or plastic bags, labelled according to the size and season they are appropriate for;

— use indelible ink to mark the sizes on the labels. It will save a lot of time measuring up and sorting through later on. It is best to do this as soon as you get the clothes.

HANGING CLOTHES

(see also Skirts, below and Wardrobes in AT BEDTIME chapter)

To stop sun-frocks and wide-necked garments slipping off the coathanger:
— wind rubber bands around each end of the hanger, so that the clothes will grip on to them;

— attach foam rubber to either end of the hanger;

— poke a drawing pin into each end of a wooden hanger to prevent the thin straps falling any further off the hanger.

HEMS *(see Jeans, this chapter)*

To prevent hems pulling and coming undone, make a tying off knot in the thread about every eight centimetres. If the hem happens to get caught while the child is playing, no more than eight centimetres should undo.

To stop the crease of an old hemline showing, sprinkle salt on the wrong side of the crease and then iron with a steam iron or with a damp cloth. Brush any excess salt away.

JEANS

To patch a pair of jeans, remove the back pocket and sew it over the worn or torn area.

To prolong the life of a pair of jeans, sew or iron a patch on the inside of each knee before they are worn.

To camouflage the white hemline after lengthening jeans:
— wipe on a little blue ink, mixed with water to obtain the correct shade;

— use a blue crayon or felt-tipped pen of the correct shade to cover the mark.

KNITTING FOR CHILDREN
(see also **Booties** *and* **Woollens,** *this chapter)*

To strengthen the elbows and prolong the life of jerseys and cardigans:
— sew a patch of cotton or two layers of pantyhose inside the sleeves at the elbows. This is especially good for school jumpers as children often lean on their elbows at their desks;

— when knitting the jersey, knit two extra patches approximately 10 cm x 15 cm and sew them on the insides of the elbows;

— when knitting the sleeve, reinforce the elbow area by knitting with two strands of wool instead of one;

— when knitting the jersey, use a reel of matching cotton to knit in with the wool around the elbow area.

To make a child's hand-knitted garment easy to lengthen when a child grows:
— when knitting the garment, cast off after knitting each band. Turn the work upside down and pick up and knit the stitches on the cast-on edge. If you keep some spare wool, you can simply undo the cast-off edge and knit some more rows;

— unpick the bands and sew on some matching stretch-fabric ribbing.

LABELS *(see* **Name Tags,** *this chapter)*

LONG PANTS *(see* **Overalls,** *this chapter)*

To extend the life of a toddler's long pants, when they have become too short, thread elastic through the hems. They will look especially cute when worn with tights.

For extra warmth and to protect the knees of a toddler's long pants, make a pair of 'leg-warmers' from a pair of adult socks. Discard the foot and heel of the sock, hem the raw edge and you have a pair of small 'leg-warmers'.

JUMPERS *(see* **Woollens,** *this chapter)*

NAME-TAGS

To help keep name-tags clear for longer, paint over them with clear nail polish.

To get lost articles back more easily, write your phone number as well as your child's name inside his clothes. When getting name-tags professionally printed, most firms only allow two names so use the family name and phone number. The name tags will then also apply when brothers and sisters wear the clothing.

Sew name tags on T shirts and stretch fabric, by stitching down the ribbing rather than across it, to prevent it breaking when stretched.

When naming very expensive items of clothing, such as school blazers, take the time to embroider the name in an unobtrusive spot, such as on the inside lining. Name tags can be cut out quite easily, but embroidering the actual garment will hopefully be more of a safe-guard against theft.

NAPPIES (see also **Plastic Pants,** this chapter)
Changing Baby's Nappies

To change baby's nappy, lay him on a mat or towel on the bathroom vanity, with his bottom near the basin. Holding baby's legs up, you will easily be able to splash his bottom with warm water from the basin. This will only be practical when your baby is very little or if there is a reasonable amount of room on one side of the basin.

To clean baby's bottom:
— keep a plastic ice cream container handy in the bathroom so that when baby soils his nappies, warm water can be brought to the changing area;
— use muslin squares (see Bathing Baby in IN THE BATHROOM chapter).

When changing baby in the middle of cold winter nights:
— warm up his nappies and spare night gown by placing them under your electric blanket while you sleep;
— keep warm water in an air pot in baby's bedroom, to save having to traipse to the bathroom each time to wash his bottom.

To help safety pins slip through nappies more easily:
— keep them poked into a bar of damp soap while they are not being used;
— lubricate them with a little petroleum jelly;
— run the sharp end of the pin through your hair before poking it into the nappy. The oil in your hair will lubricate it.

To make it easier for you to change baby's nappies:
— buy clothes that have zips or press studs right down one leg;
— dress newborn babies in night-gowns as much as possible in the

first few weeks when they need their nappies changed the most. It is easy to lift up the gown to change his pants. If the weather is cold, leggings can be worn underneath.

When your toddler detests having his nappies changed:
— try to get him as relaxed as possible before attempting to change him;

— try to get as much eye contact as possible while telling him funny stories and making funny faces;

— play at changing his teddy's or doll's nappies and praise the doll for not moving about.

To make it easier to clean a baby's dirty bottom, use petroleum jelly or barrier cream on the skin when changing. This will also help to prevent nappy rash.

To remove the odour of a dirty nappy, strike a match after changing.

Disposable Nappies

To stick down disposable nappies which have lost their tapes, use pieces of masking tape.

Dry your hands after using lotions and creams before sticking down the tape, when using disposable nappies. Any residue of cream on the plastic will prevent the tape sticking. Keep a hand towel next to the changing table to wipe your hands on after using the creams.

To make a disposable nappy more absorbent for night time, place a cloth nappy, folded to form a pad, down the centre of the opened disposable nappy. The tapes will hold them both on securely and you won't need to use plastic pants. Use a nappy liner on top of the nappy pad if there is a chance that it may be dirtied.

When using disposable nappies that are gathered around the leg, use your finger to gently even out the gathers after the nappy has been put on. This will make it more comfortable.

To be prepared, keep one or two spare disposable nappies and a plastic bag:
— at grandma's house or at the house of people you regularly visit;

— in the glove compartment of the car.

Keep a few spare disposable nappies to use in the following ways:
— as a protective pad to place under baby's bottom when you have to change his nappies on your lap or while you are out;

— if you have a particularly 'spilling' baby, fold a disposable nappy over your shoulder (inside out) when burping baby after a feed.

When an older child, who only wears a disposable nappy for a daytime sleep, is wearing long pants, leave their underpants on, on top of the nappy. This will make it much easier to simply slip the nappy off when they wake up.

Drying Nappies

To prevent too many wrinkles forming when drying fabric nappies (towelling nappies don't usually wrinkle too much):
— use a gentle spin cycle in the washing machine;

— remove the nappies immediately the dryer stops. If you have left them in for longer, put a damp towel in the dryer with them and tumble again for a few minutes. They will be easier to fold neatly. However, make sure they are never damp when using.

To soften towelling nappies, which have become hard and crunchy from being continually dried on a clothes' line, try drying them once or twice in a clothes' dryer to fluff them up. Continual drying in a clothes' dryer, however, will cause them to wear out quicker and dirty stains will not disappear as easily when not hung in the sun.

Hanging Nappies On The Line

To save bending while hanging nappies on the line:
— keep pegs in an old shoulder bag, which can be worn over one shoulder or around your neck;

— if you don't have a trundler for the clothes' basket, place it on top of a rubbish bin or wheelbarrow.

To save space on the clothesline:
— peg a row of nappies on the line and then use spring pegs to pin another row of nappies to the bottoms of the first row;

— peg nappies from line to line. One corner of the nappy would be pegged to the outside line and the other pegged to the parallel line next to it in a zig zag pattern. This also stops them wrapping around each other on windy days. Towels and tea towels can be hung in the same way.

To make more room to dry nappies indoors, hang two coathangers over your shower-curtain rod, the width of a nappy apart. Pin the corners of six or seven nappies to one coathanger and the opposite corners of the same nappies to the second coathanger. You will be able to dry about six nappies in the space normally taken to hang one.

Nappy Bag

When you arrive home from an outing, repack your nappy bag so that it will be ready for next time.

To make it easy to carry your nappy bag on your pram handles, sew short straps to the top of the bag at either end of the zip. Sew strong press studs on to these straps so they can be clipped over the handles of the pram. **Note:** Don't hang heavy bags on light strollers!

If you use plastic bags to put soiled nappies in, be careful not to let babies and toddlers get near them.

Nappy Buckets

Use a medium-sized plastic rubbish bin, with a tight-fitting lid, as a nappy bucket. It is cheaper and will hold more.

A useful substitute for a nappy bucket is a tall plastic kitchen tidy with a swinging lid. It is always important to keep nappy buckets well out of reach of children, but this style, in particular, must be inaccessible to any mobile babies or toddlers in the house who could investigate it.

Use old nappy buckets, which have been sterilised, for storing children's blocks and toys in.

Nappy Rash

If your baby is suffering from nappy rash:
— put about ½ cup white vinegar in the final rinsing water when washing the nappies. Don't spin all the water out before placing them on the line, preferably in the sun, to dry;

— dry her bottom with the warm air of a hair dryer, as a towel or cloth can irritate the sensitive skin. Hold the dryer at least 10 cm from the skin and don't use hot air;

— add ¼ cup baking soda to 10 cm bath water. This helps to soften the water.

Recycling Nappies

When nappies have become very thin, keep them to use as liner pads for night nappies. Just fold them into a pad and sit them on top of the folded nappy with the nappy liner on top of that.

Stains On Nappies

To remove stains on nappies, resulting from using zinc-based creams, soak the nappy in a bucket filled with hot water and about 1 tablespoon bicarbonate of soda. After a few hours wash it with soap powder and one more tablespoon bicarbonate of soda.

To bleach dirty nappies, hang them on the line in the sun. The sun will bleach and sterilise them.

Washing Nappies
(see Hanging Nappies on the Line, this chapter)

To clean off dirty nappies, before washing:
— keep an old, blunt knife handy in the bathroom to use for scraping off any deposits on the nappy before soaking. Use indelible ink to write 'Nappies only' on it and keep it out of reach of toddlers;

— use an old dish brush with 'Nappies only' written on it.

To soften nappies and to keep them smelling fresh, add ½ cup bicarbonate of soda to your machine's second washing cycle. It will not cause irritation to the skin.

To save having to put your hands in the nappy solution:
— use a pair of plastic tongs;

— keep an old pair of rubber gloves next to the bucket to slip on when emptying it;

— use an old wooden spoon to mix up the solution and to stir the nappies in the solution. Write 'Nappies only' on the handle!

OVERALLS, CRAWLERS *(see Dressing Babies, this chapter)*

Overalls and crawlers are normally thought of as winter clothing. However, **if you have a baby who is at the crawling stage in the warmer part of the year,** consider making some long-legged crawlers out of light, cool fabric. They make for much more comfortable 'crawling' and saves baby getting too dirty.

To keep newborn's tiny feet in the feet of crawlers or all-in-one suits (when they bend their knees up their feet often lift up into the leg part), put a pair of booties or socks on their feet either underneath or on top of the leggings.

To remove that 'cold gap' around the crawling baby's middle, as jumpers and sweat shirts ride up, dress him in an all-in-one singlet or stretchy rompersuit underneath his crawlers. This will also stop the nappy from working its way off.

Invest in a pair of braces for your toddler. They come in really handy when trying to hold up a pair of crawlers or long pants, especially if the pants are too big or the elastic has worn.

To make overalls last longer, sew a little pocket inside each knee and place a small square of foam rubber in it. The rubber can be removed when the overalls are put in the wash.

To make it easier to alter overalls when they become too small, sew the buttons on the straps rather than the bib.

Use parka nylon to make a pair of overalls for a toddler to wear outside. They will keep him dry and warm and will be easily washed.

PLASTIC PANTS

To dry a pair of baby's plastic pants in a hurry, use a hair dryer.

To prevent plastic pants becoming hard and cracking, add a little baby oil to the water to soften the plastic.

When the plastic has perished in fabric-covered plastic pants, cut out the plastic and use the fabric pants to put on babies over disposable nappies or plain plastic pants. They look more attractive than the plain plastic.

PYJAMAS AND NIGHTIES

To prevent holes forming behind buttons in pyjamas, sew the facing behind the buttons to the body of the pyjama top. This will strengthen the fabric.

If the button holes are too big and the pyjama coat keeps coming undone:
— do the buttons up and sew the two sides together, leaving just enough at the top for it to be taken off and on over the child's head;

— use a zig zag stitch on the edges of the buttonholes to decrease their size.

If all-in-one pyjama suits become too short:
— cut off the feet and put a false hem around the bottom;

— cut off the feet and sew on a pair of socks. This will both lengthen the legs and enlarge the feet.

If the feet of your children's all-in-one pyjama suits begin to wear out, reinforce the feet with iron-on patches.

When making winter pyjamas for toddlers:
— make the pants into overalls which can hold the pyjama top in place without leaving any gaps for them to get cold;

— knit woollen cuffs at wrists and ankles to ensure a snug fit.

For added warmth in winter, make a warm all-in-one 'blanket sleeper suit' for your children to wear on top of their pyjamas. This will be especially useful for children who always kick off their bed covers.

If you find the feet difficult to make, just sew a pair of warm socks on to the legs.

To keep children's backs covered at night:
— pin their pyjama tops to their pyjama pants;

— sew buttons and button holes around the middle of children's pyjamas;

— put an all-in-one singlet, or towelling romper suit, on the child underneath the pyjamas. These singlets, which button together between the legs, can be bought for babies and toddlers.

Nighties for newborns will be extra warm in winter if you:
— put a draw-string around the bottom. You will be able to open it up to change nappies and close it to keep the warm air in;

— sew them across the bottom to make a sleeping bag. This idea is suitable with large nighties that undo right down the back or front, so that you can still have easy access to the nappy.

If you sew your children's nightwear, make sure you check that you use low-fire risk fabric and styles. Flowing nighties look nice but are a fire risk.

RAINCOATS

To make a raincoat easily identifiable and visible to motorists, use reflective tape to make a unique design on the coat. Your child will stand out in a crowd and on the road!

To mend a tear in a lightweight raincoat, use masking tape.

Raincoats that are torn or too small can be used as follows:
— cut up to make a gym bag or swimming bag for children;

— a cape for home hairdressing;

— a cover-all apron for children when they are painting.

SEWING CHILDREN'S CLOTHES

(see also **Individual Garments,** this chapter)

Applique

To prevent applique from wrinkling, when sewing it on to garments, dip the piece into a weak starch solution and while it is still wet, iron it in place, before using a zigzag stitch to sew around the outside.

To make fancy applique pieces for clothing, use one of the following methods:
— trace around the fancy shapes of biscuit cutters;

— trace around the shapes of children's stencils;

— trace pictures from colouring-in books.

Braid, Lace and Rickrack

Before sewing braid, lace or seam binding onto a garment, wash it first to save shrinkage and puckering later.

To make it easier to sew laces and braids onto fabric, stick it in place first with sticky tape. Sew right over the tape and remove it afterwards.

To prevent rick-rack curling, sew it onto the garment with a zigzag stitch.

Buttons *(see also* Buttons *and* Pyjamas, *this chapter)*

To ensure you have a spare button, buy one extra and sew it to an inconspicuous part of the garment, such as the hemline, on the inside of the pocket or under the collar.

To keep four-holed buttons in place longer, sew each pair of holes separately, breaking the thread between each side. Paint the stitched thread with clear nail polish.

To reinforce fabric under buttons, cut a small square of fabric or tape and place it between the facing and garment. Sew the button into place, stitching through all three layers of fabric. A long piece of tape can be used instead to sew down the inside of the button band.

When sewing buttonholes on children's garments, sew them horizontally rather than vertically and the buttons won't come undone as easily.

Elastic

To easily replace elastic, attach the new elastic to the end of the old elastic before pulling it through.

SHAWLS

To store a woollen baby's shawl:
— wrap it in blue tissue paper, to keep it white and then wrap that in newspaper to keep away the moths. Store it in a dry, dark place, but open it up every few months to air it and give it a shake;

— roll it up and put it into a large, dry glass jar with a plastic screw-top lid. Roll the jar in plenty of newspaper and keep it in a dark place.

SHIRTS AND BLOUSES

When making long sleeves on small children's shirts and blouses, thread shirring elastic through the hems of the sleeves at the cuffs, instead of fastening them with buttons. It will be easier for the children to dress themselves and they will be able to pull their sleeves up when playing with paints, water and other messy things.

SHOES
Babies' Shoes

To put shoes and socks on a toddler who won't sit still, sit him in a high chair or stroller and give him something to play with.

To make it easier for small children to put on their shoes, use nail polish or a permanent marker to put a mark on the inside of the right shoe only.

To help a baby feel more secure when learning to walk, glue a very thin strip of foam plastic or rubber to the soles of both shoes. He will not slip over as easily.

Canvas Shoes

To help white canvas shoes resist grass stains, spray them with hair spray.

To clean canvas shoes, put them in the washing machine on a cool wash.

To clean badly marked tennis shoes, rub them over with a wet soap-filled, steelo pad.

To make new fabric shoes last longer, spray them with a fabric protector before you wear them. White tennis shoes should be sprayed with starch before they are worn.

Cleaning Shoes

To make it easier for children to clean and polish their own shoes, keep each different coloured shoe polish separate in its own plastic bag, along with the appropriate brushes, cloths and polishing pads.

To make it easier for children to clean their sandals and shoes without getting into too much of a mess, get them to put their hand inside a plastic bag, sock or paper bag before putting it into the shoe.

To help children clean mud off their shoes, tack a metal bottle top to the back of the shoe-polishing brush, to scrape the mud off with.

To polish patent leather shoes:
— smear some petroleum jelly on a cloth and rub it over the shoes.

Polish it off with a clean cloth;

— use spray-on furniture polish or use paper towel to apply undiluted vinyl floor cleaning solution. It will dry straight away and protect the shoes as well.

To cover up scratch marks on children's shoes, paint over the damaged area with a matching felt-tip pen.

To remove scuff marks from white shoes:
— put some typewriter correction fluid on the mark before polishing the shoes;

— clean the marks off with a little liquid scourer on a paper towel. Rinse off before polishing the shoes;

— rub over the marks with a little nail polish remover before polishing with white shoe polish.

To remove scuff marks from black shoes, apply a little india ink before polishing.

To remove greasy marks from shoes, use oil of eucalyptus.

Gumboots

To prevent chafing and to keep children's feet warm, glue small scraps of sheepskin around the inside tops of children's gumboots.

To help children to identify their own gumboots:
— cut two identical shapes from coloured reflecting tape and stick one on the back of each boot;

— write the child's first name in large capital letters inside the left boot and his last name in large capital letters inside the right boot. When the boots are placed together in the correct order, the child will easily see which boot belongs on which foot. Write the other part of his name in small letters underneath the large writing, so that if one boot is misplaced, the owner will be easily identified;

— use pearly nail polish to label the outside of the gumboots, for quick identification.

When children wear gumboots to school, give them a spring clothes' peg, with their name on it, to clip their gumboots together when they take them off. This will save them getting mixed up with everybody else's.

New Shoes

To prevent blistered heels caused by new shoes, keep rubbing a little soap on the inside heel of each shoe during the period in which your child is breaking in the shoes.

To prevent children slipping while wearing new leather-soled shoes:
— rub the soles with an emery board or sand paper;

— rub the soles over a rough concrete surface or a brick.

Sandals

To prevent socks being stained by children's sandals, paint over the insides of the sandals with clear varnish before they are worn.

Shoe Laces

To untangle knotted shoe laces, try using a pair of tweezers.

To repair shoe laces which have lost their tips, dip them in clear nail polish or glue and shape them into a point. Allow them to dry before using.

To prevent loss of shoe laces, tie a knot on both sides of the lace after threading it through either the first or last set of holes in the shoe.

To help leather shoe laces stay tied up longer, sprinkle a few drops of water on the knot when tying it.

Storing Shoes

To store the family's shoes and boots tidily in wet weather or if you prefer people not to wear shoes inside the house:
— have some shelves in the garage next to the inside door or on the back porch for everybody's shoes. If they are all kept together in their own separate space or shelf they should not get misplaced. Slippers or indoor shoes can be left in the space when you go out, ready to change into before going back inside;

— keep an old plastic vegetable stacker near the door and allocate one basket for each member of the family to put their shoes in when entering the house.

Wet Shoes (see Storing Shoes, prior entry)

To protect school shoes which get water-logged, rub candle wax around the stitching at the base of the uppers.

To dry soaked leather shoes, stuff them with newspaper. This will help them to keep their shape. Dry them away from the direct heat of fires and heaters so as not to crack the leather.

To encourage children (and adults!) to get rid of mud or dirt from their shoes before entering the house, place a brick by the entrance for them to scrape their shoes on before taking them off.

SINGLETS

Instead of singlets in winter, dress your babies and toddlers in stretchy rompersuits underneath clothes that may expose their 'middle'.

SKIRTS

To hang skirts and trousers, use a normal coathanger with a large bulldog clip attached at either end.

To help pleats on skirts sit better, machine down the edge of each pleat on the wrong side. The stitching will not show.

To make it easier to iron pleats, hold them together with paper-clips.

If your child's waistband is too loose on her skirt or long pants, thread elastic through the back waistband from the side seams.

To make a skirt warmer for winter, sew the skirt to a short-sleeved T-shirt. It makes a comfortable, warm bodice, and will save you or your daughter having to do up any buttons. An old singlet can be used in the same way.

To extend the life of a skirt on a bodice, make the bodice longer than required and take two large tucks right around it. As your daughter grows, the tucks can be let down and should allow many years' wear.

SOCKS

Buy several pairs of socks the same for each child, so that when you gradually lose them, you will still be able to make up some pairs.

Keep odd socks to be worn:
— inside gumboots;

— as bed socks.

If your children insist on pulling or kicking off their socks or booties at night:
— use a large tacking stitch to sew them to their pyjamas;

— put thick tights on them, underneath their pyjama pants.

To save hunting for the special pair of socks that goes with a particular outfit, pin the socks to the garment while it hangs in the wardrobe.

Sew matching lace or trims to your little girl's **socks to coordinate them with her clothes.**

To stretch woollen socks which have shrunk, put a golf ball or a bottle inside the socks and hang them on the line to dry.

Remember that tight-fitting socks can damage feet.

Cut the tops off socks and use them to make warm cuffs for children's pyjama pants and sleeves. Sew them on when the pyjamas become too small.

SUN HATS

If your child's sunhat doesn't have a flap to cover the neck, pin a handkerchief to the back of the hat.

UNIFORMS

If your children wear school uniforms, get them into the habit of checking over their uniforms each afternoon when they change out of them, to see whether anything needs ironing or mending and to see that shoes are clean etc. They should either bring these things to your attention then or fix the problem themselves, so there are no last minute panics in the morning.

When hemming school uniforms, only sew about five centimetres of hem at a time. Tie a knot and start with a new piece of thread for another five centimetres and so on. If your daughter puts her foot in her hem or gets it caught while playing, only a small amount will undo.

To sew a large number of cloth badges on to a uniform, tack the badges to the uniform and use an invisible thread in the sewing machine to quickly sew them all on at once with a zig zag stitch around the edges. This is ideal for Brownie badges and souvenir badges.

To clean metal badges for Brownies and Cubs, use toothpaste on an old toothbrush.

WASHING CHILDREN'S CLOTHES (see also **Booties,** this chapter)

To remember when clothes need special treatment for stains:
— tie the stained part of the piece of clothing in a loose knot. Seeing the knot will remind you to treat the stain;

— clip a peg to the stained area. When you come to put it in the washing machine, you will be reminded that special treatment is required. Teach your children to do this for you.

To brighten up baby's white clothes, soak them in cold water first and then wash them in a warm nappy-soaking solution. Rinse thoroughly.

To dry delicate garments when there is no shade available, put up a sun umbrella and use the stays to hang the coat hangers on or to clip the pegs on to.

WOOLLENS (see also Knitting for Children, above)

When dressing a small baby in an open, lacy knitted garment, put a pair of socks over her hands to save her little fingers getting caught in the pattern.

To tighten the bottom of a jumper which has stretched, thread a bodkin with flat, narrow elastic and thread it through the 'knit' stitches at the bottom of the garment on the wrong side. Adjust the jumper to fit and join the edges together neatly.

If the sleeves on a child's cardigan are too long, cut off the sleeves and sew on stretch ribbing.

To dry jumpers and cardigans more quickly, place a long cardboard roll, from the inside of a lunch-wrap, in each sleeve before laying it down to dry.

To keep children warm without having to hand-wash woollens all the time, knit sleeveless vests for the children to wear over a singlet, and underneath a sweat shirt. The sweat shirt is far more easily washed.

To prevent fluffy bobbles forming on woollens:
— turn them inside out before washing;

— if washing in the machine, make sure there is plenty of room for them to move around so they won't rub against themselves;

— if hand-washing, do not rub them together.

To remove fluff and bobbles from woollens:
— rub gently over the garment with a regular razor or an electric razor;

— rub over the garment with fine sandpaper.

A child's cardigan can be used as a hot-water bottle cover, when it is too small or worn out. Remove the sleeves and sew up the armholes and around the bottom. The hot-water bottle can be placed inside and buttoned up.

ZIPS

To help a child who finds zips difficult to do up:
— attach a key-ring loop to the metal tag on the zip for the little fingers to grasp;

— attach a short piece of cord or ribbon to the tag on the zip.

HASSLE-FREE LIVING WITH KIDS...
Development

(see also IN FAMILIES chapter)

BAD HABITS *(see Thumb-sucking, this chapter)*

When trying to break a child's bad habit, incentives are usually necessary. Small children have difficulty looking beyond the present, to a 'reward at the end of the week', so an immediate reward is important. Buy lots of inexpensive little treats (preferably not food) to wrap up and put into a bucket filled with sawdust or sand, to make a 'lucky dip'. When a child has performed well, e.g. gone a whole night without getting up or lasted a whole day without fighting, they can dip into the bucket for their reward. To save this exercise becoming too expensive, tell your children that there are a certain number of treats in the bucket (don't say how many) and when they have all gone, that's it! Hopefully the habit will be broken before the bucket is empty. Once a certain degree of success has been accomplished, you may be able to offer a larger treat for a longer period of success and perhaps a generous treat, such as a trip to the zoo, when success has stretched over a period of a week or two.

COORDINATION (see Coordination in AT PLAY chapter)

CRYING (see Irritable Children, this chapter)

To try to soothe an irritable and restless baby, after checking that all her obvious requirements have been met:
— play some quiet, soothing music;

— leave some quiet, low humming noise in her room, such as a fan, a vacuum cleaner, an aquarium or an untuned radio;

— stroke her cheek while looking in her eyes and talking gently;

— rock her in her bassinet. When rocking the bassinet, it should not be too slow, but about sixty rocks per minute;

— walk around the room with her over your shoulder or take her for a walk in your arms around the garden;

— gently rub her earlobe between your finger and thumb;

— rock her in your arms or in a swing;

— give her a warm, relaxing bath by herself or with you. You may need to relax in a bath too, by this stage;

— give her a gentle massage;

— take her for a walk in the pram;

— take her for a ride in the car;

— place her gently in her cot with lots of interesting things to look at around the room. Mobiles can be a great distraction for an unsettled baby. Place something in her room that will make a constant burring sound, such as a fan or a fan heater.

To try to stop your child crying, try one of the following:
— start whispering a happy message in his ear. The child will need to stop crying to hear what you are saying and will hopefully calm down as a result;

— get a special little bottle to put all the tears in. Let her know that you can't waste one tear and hold it ready to collect them. (Of course, if the child is very distressed and throwing herself around, this would not be the safest thing to do);

— hold her in front of the mirror so she will be able to see all her tears. She may get so interested in where they are running to that she forgets to keep crying!

If your baby holds his breath while crying:
— blow lightly on his face;

— gently raise the infant's arms straight above his head. This will expand the lungs and force the child to draw a breath;

— place a cool, damp cloth on his face.

DUMMIES

If your baby sucks a dummy, make sure you have at least one spare. As soon as one drops on the ground or gets dirty in some way, it can be replaced with a clean one from the sterilising solution.

If your baby enjoys sucking a dummy, tie a short ribbon on to the dummy and pin it to her clothing (don't use a long ribbon as it could cause an accident if it wraps around baby's neck). If it drops, it will not touch the floor, so she will not have to wait while it is sterilised or replaced and you won't have to wait as long for baby to settle down again!

For a baby who keeps losing his dummy at night, buy a luminous 'glow-in-the-dark' dummy, to help him find it more easily in the cot.

Never allow your baby to suck a dummy that has been dipped in something sweet! That is one of the worst things you can do for his developing teeth.

To help a toddler break the habit of sucking a dummy:
— every few days cut off a little piece of the dummy. As it shrinks, the less desirable it will become, hopefully!

— use a special occasion to 'give the dummy away', e.g. to Santa Claus or to a friend's new baby! It sometimes helps a toddler to come to grips with giving it up if she can actually give it away and talk about it;

— tell your little one that when this particular dummy is lost or worn out, there will be no replacement.

FEARS

When dealing with children who have specific fears:
— don't make them feel stupid. Remember back to your childhood and try to understand the situation from the child's point of view;

— don't become tense and upset over the situation. Your child needs you to be calm and comforting;

— never force your child into a situation that he is terrified of.

Fear of the Dark

To help children who have a fear of the dark, take them out for a walk just before dusk. Talk about the different colours in the sky as the sun goes down and when it gets dark, look at things by torchlight. See how many 'night time things' you can talk about, e.g. aeroplanes at night, lights turning on, moths, animals etc.

Fear of Thunder

To help children who have a fear of thunder:
— talk about it in a light-hearted way, discussing and imitating the loud noise;

— they usually feel scared because the thunder has given them a fright. Next time there is a heavy storm say 'I wonder whether there will be some thunder in this storm. We won't be scared today because we know it may come';

— tell them that you can usually see lightning before thunder and when the sky flashes start counting slowly until the thunder comes. Make a game out of it.

INDEPENDENCE

To encourage independence in small children, have them with you at times when you are getting everything ready for a bath, going to bed, going out etc. Talk to them about what you are doing so that before long they will be able to get themselves ready.

IRRITABLE CHILDREN *(see Crying, this chapter)*

If baby has a difficult period during the day or evening, choose that time to give her a soothing, warm bath before putting her down to sleep. A warm bath may sometimes make a baby too relaxed to want to feed properly so if you find her dropping off to sleep after a bath while you are trying to feed her, it may pay to re-schedule her routine. However, it is not good to bath a baby immediately after feeding.

KEYS

If your child lets himself in the house and has his own set of keys, make it easier for him to find the right one by painting a dot on each key to match the colour of something to do with the door it is for, e.g. a white dot for the white front door, a red dot for the ranch slider door that has red curtains covering it.

KINDERGARTEN

To help prepare a child for kindergarten and pre-school:
— talk positively about what the child will be doing at kindergarten;

— give her some practice at eating from a lunch box so that she knows how to unwrap her lunch, undo her drink bottle etc. It could all be too much if on the first day she doesn't manage to balance her lunch box well on her lap, she has difficulty untangling her packet of sandwiches and all her food drops on the ground!

LEFT AND RIGHT (see Gumboots in AND THEIR CLOTHES chapter)

To reduce some of the difficulty for a child when learning Left and Right:

— from a very early age, refer to left and right as if the child understood it. e.g. 'you write with your right hand' (of course show them which one you mean) or 'open up the cupboard on the left'. Consistently referring to left and right will help a child to finally catch on;

— show older children that if they cannot remember which is which, to hold up their hands (as if to give a 'stop' signal), with the fingers straight up and their thumbs at right angles to their fingers. The left hand will make an 'L' for 'left' between the thumb and the first finger;

— encourage children to lift the appropriate hand every time you refer to left or right. Making it into a game will help them to come to grips with which is which.

LISTENING (see Listening Games in AT PLAY chapter)

To encourage your children to develop mature listening skills, teach them by example:

— endeavour to look at and listen to your children when they talk to you;

— show your interest in what they have to say by commenting about it, smiling, nodding and asking further questions;

— listen to a story or a record together;

— try to be patient when listening to a faltering speaker and resist the temptation to finish off what you think he is trying to say;

— set aside specific time each day to listen to each child. Ask them open-ended questions (not simply questions that can be answered by 'yes' or 'no'), to get them started, about something that interests them. Make a conscious effort to give them all your attention, without fidgeting, looking at your watch, looking around the room and so on.

Knowing that you are interested in what your children have to say will also strengthen their self-esteem.

Remember that at each child's age and development, they are only capable of taking in a certain amount at a time. **To encourage children to listen and understand what you are saying:**
— speak with a pleasant voice, so they want to hear what you are saying;

— don't give too many instructions at once;

— give the instructions in simple, clear language;

— make sure the television or radio is not competing for your child's attention at the same time;

— when telling toddlers what to do, use actions to show what you mean.

To encourage your children's cooperation:
— invite little ones to help, rather than always telling them what to do, e.g. let's put this cushion back on the chair. Grandma leaves it there to make the chair look nice;

— use a little humour to gain your child's enthusiasm;

— carry through with promised rewards and don't threaten to do anything for bad behaviour that you don't intend following through.

MANNERS

To teach a child good table manners:
-- from a very young age, show your children that once they have left the table, there is no more food!

— when helping a baby or toddler to feed himself, talk about the way things should be done in a way that makes him want to join in, e.g. 'We put our spoon in this hand so we can scoop up the potato like a big bulldozer'.

— if a child simply forgets his manners, rather than reprimanding him all the time for his bad manners, try to get your message across in a fairly light-hearted way, e.g. when he next asks for something without saying 'please', perhaps answer him by saying 'Are you a little boy from down the road? I thought I had Timothy at the table here, but it can't be because everyone in Timothy's family always says 'please' when they ask for something. What's your name?'

When expecting good behaviour from your children at the table, include the children in conversation from time to time so they don't get bored. Boredom can cause children to embark on behaviour that they otherwise would not take part in.

MATCHES

Store matches and lighters in a cool, dry place well out of reach of children. While children are too young to handle matches, try not to use them in front of them as this will only make them inquisitive. When they reach school age, teach them the correct way to light a match and the dangers involved in playing with them. Instruct them that they must always ask before striking a match. Allow them only to use matches under your supervision. Hopefully this will discourage secret and dangerous experiments with their friends.

MONEY (see Bus Fares in AT SCHOOL chapter)

To encourage children to earn money for themselves, suggest some of the following:
— doing odd jobs for their neighbours;

— selling some of their toys when you have a garage sale.

Children who think that they are old enough to have an allowance, but have difficulty coping with the value of cash, benefit from having a home 'bank book'. This system means that the money never leaves the parents' bank account until the child decides to spend it on something. A small note book can be drawn up to resemble a pass book. Columns for the date, 'in' and 'out' and a note to say what it was for, if it was given as a reward. A regular amount can be agreed on and written in each week. The child can be encouraged to select an item they wish to purchase from an advertising leaflet and then save for this amount. The goal needs to be obtainable in a reasonably short period of time for young children. Specific rules for your particular family can be laid down, e.g. fines to be paid for not doing chores or bonuses for doing extra jobs. Small amounts of interest can be given when the child is saving extra hard and interest could be charged for loans so that the child comes to the realisation of the value of his money. Although this will take a little time to implement, it should certainly discourage your children spending all their money on lollies!

PROBLEM SOLVING
(see also **Stranger Danger** in **ON OUTINGS** chapter)

To encourage children to think about how they would solve practical problems, play a 'What if?' game. Give the children practical problems to solve which require mature reasoning. For instance, 'What if you were to get home from school and there was no-one there?' 'What if you dropped a plate of butter upside down on the floor?' 'What if you got separated from your parents while out shopping?' This can be a valuable opportunity to guide your children and in a way that is fun for them.

REMINDERS

Keep a different-coloured clip peg for each member of the family on some hooks or on a magnet on the refrigerator. Reminders, library cards, school notices, lunch money etc can be clipped on to these and each person will know to check their clip regularly.

To remind children when to do things, have a toy clock next to a real clock and tell them that when the clocks are the same it will be time to pack up their toys or come for dinner etc. This is also a good way to reduce continuous questions about when a favourite television show will be on or when daddy or mummy will be home from work.

SECURITY BLANKETS

To stop a security blanket being dragged around in the dirt, cut it in half. This will enable you to wash one piece while the other is being treasured. If you gradually keep cutting pieces off the blanket, your toddler may lose interest in it altogether.

SELF-ESTEEM *(see* IN FAMILIES *chapter)*

SHARING

To encourage your children to share swings, bikes, toys etc:
— use an egg-timer to give them turns of equal length. If the activities require longer turns, use the timer on the stove;
— ask them to suggest the fairest solution to the problem.

To discourage selfishness, have the children understand that whoever says 'me first' is automatically last!

To teach children how important it is to share, show them situations in everyday life where people are required to share, such as family meal times. Seeing other people sharing will help them to realise that you don't miss out when sharing with someone else, especially when it is done happily.

When first teaching little ones to share things, give them something to replace the toy that is being shared. Say 'swap' while handing him something with one hand and gently extracting the 'required toy' from the other.

Children should be excused from sharing one or two very special toys or belongings if they don't want to, but these should be kept out of the way of others who may be tempted to play with them. This will help them to appreciate that some things can be 'sacred' and special to themselves.

SHOPPING *(see also* ON OUTINGS *chapter)*

To help children remember what to buy when they go shopping by themselves:

— cut old cereal boxes up into strips to write shopping lists on. They will be much easier than paper for children to handle and a hole can be poked in one end for a piece of string to go through so it can be tied to a shopping bag;

— put the shopping list inside a plastic luggage label and tie that to their shopping bag, belt or purse.

SPEECH

When talking to babies:

— speak clearly, slowly and in simple terms;

— try to illustrate what you are saying by pointing to the things you are talking about and making actions to convey what you are saying.

To encourage a toddler to talk:

— keep your sentences short and simple so that he will not be too put off by the difficulty of speech;

— ask him to say what he wants when he makes gestures with his hands, especially if he knows the word to use;

— listen to them when they want to talk, so they realise that what they have to say is important;

— when reading a story, saying a rhyme or singing a song that he knows, stop occasionally for him to fill in the word.

When your child says things incorrectly, don't emphasise his mistake but just rephrase what he has said in the correct way, e.g. if he says 'dink', say 'Tom wants a drink?' or if he says 'the bird flying sky', you could say 'yes, the birds are flying in the sky'.

TEETHING

To provide your baby with a little relief when teething, give one of the following:

— a frozen banana;

— a frozen teat. Fill a sterilised teat with water and freeze it. Screw it on to the bottle and give it to baby to suck on;

— a piece of frozen orange. Remove the peel and pips from the orange, wrap individual segments in plastic wrap and put them in the freezer. The vitamin C is a bonus!

— half a rusk. Cut in half lengthwise, to avoid wastage and to make it easier for baby to hold;

— an ice cube. Tie some ice in the corner of a clean handkerchief and give it to your baby. He will automatically suck or chew on it.

If baby finds breastfeeding painful, while teething, express a little before she starts to feed so she doesn't have to work too hard to get the milk flowing.

If baby dribbles a lot while teething, put a little petroleum jelly around his chin and cheeks to stop them becoming too sore.

TELEPHONES

To prevent young children taking telephones off the hook, place a large, wide rubber band around the telephone from the top to the bottom, over the receiver buttons to hold them down.

To teach a young child his telephone number and address, sing it to him to the tune of an easy nursery rhyme. He'll learn it quickly. Assure your little one that if he ever gets lost and needs to recall his telephone number, he can do it by singing that song.

To teach your child whom to telephone in emergencies, have a card handy to the telephone with the names and numbers of neighbours, relatives and emergency services clearly written on it in bold letters. If the child is too young to read words, but can recognise numbers, stick on to the card appropriate pictures of daddy, fire, a doctor, grandma and so on.

If you have a telephone with a memory system, draw a small different coloured dot on each of the memory numbers that your young children might need in an emergency, e.g. yellow for nana, blue for daddy, red for fire brigade etc. Have a card beside the telephone with photographs or pictures of all these people with the correct coloured dot beside it. An infant will be able to recognise the right colour to push before he is able to recognise numbers. It is a good idea to do this if mother is sick at home.

THUMB-SUCKING

When trying to discourage thumb-sucking:
— distract a baby or toddler by offering her a toy or something to play with when the thumb goes in the mouth;

— draw a picture on her thumb of her favourite animal or cartoon character. Say to the child 'Mickey Mouse' doesn't really want to be put in your mouth. You wouldn't want to upset Mickey, would you?'

— tell an older child that before she sucks her thumb she should wash her hands. When you see the thumb heading towards the mouth, ask her to go to wash her hands and this may distract her for a time;

— allow an older child to only suck her thumb when in bed or to comfort her when in the car. If you see her sucking her thumb while watching television or at some other time, say that she may suck it, but she must lie down on her bed to do so;

— try to get another adult to speak to her about thumb-sucking while she is in a group. She won't feel as embarrassed if it is not aimed at her and children often like to do what other adults say!

TIME

To help a child develop the concept of time:
— speak about the order in which things happen during the day, e.g. breakfast time, lunch time, sleep time, afternoon tea time, bath time, dinner time etc;

— use words such as, first, second and last;

— refer to time when you talk about things, e.g. 'we will go to playgroup before lunch', 'you saw Michael's daddy at kindergarten yesterday', 'we will leave the bike in the shed until we play with it again tomorrow' etc.

Have your children arrange pictures in a logical sequence. Cut some simple cartoons or a sequence of pictures out of a magazine and get them to arrange them according to what happened 'first', 'next', 'after that' and 'at the end'.

TOILET TRAINING

(see also Toilets *in* IN THE BATHROOM *chapter)*

When teaching a child to use the toilet, train them right from the start to wash their hands after each visit. Although this can be a hassle at the time, it will save having to re-train later on.

To help a toddler feel more secure on the 'big toilet':
— supply a small seat to put on top of the big toilet seat;

— have a small stool or box for him to put his feet on;

— make sure no one ever flushes the toilet while he is sitting on it!

To encourage a reluctant toddler to use the toilet:
— place a ping pong ball in the toilet bowl for your little boy to aim at;

— screw up two or three little pieces of toilet paper and suggest that your little boy tries to sink the 'ships'.

— encourage your toddler to go to the toilet or the potty at the same time as you go;

— praise your child for his successes and make it an enjoyable time for him by happily clapping your hands and dancing around.

If you have a toddler who likes to say 'no' to everything you suggest:
— rather than ask 'do you want to go to the toilet?', say 'would you like me to help you or do you want to go to the toilet yourself?' When given an option about something they are not as likely to say 'No!';

— if you have more than one toilet in your house, ask Junior if she wants to go to the upstairs toilet or the downstairs toilet.

Keep a potty with you when travelling in the car, so your child will be able to go by just stopping on the side of the road. She will probably manage to use the potty on the floor of the back seat.

To encourage a child to stop wetting his or her pants:
— tell the child that if they would like to wear proper pants, they will need to use the toilet;

— give them a very special pair of underpants, preferably with a picture of a person or animal on them. Tell them that they shouldn't really wet the pants because they don't want the little girl or dog to get wet.

To encourage an older child, who frequently wets the bed, to keep dry at night, make or buy for him or her a very special pair of pyjamas. A plain pair of pyjamas could be dressed up with appliques of the child's favourite animal, toy, car, ballet dancer, footballer etc. For a little girl, you could add lots of frills and perhaps racing stripes for a boy. Show the pyjamas to the child, who is bound to want to wear them. Explain that they can't wear these special pyjamas yet, because they would get wet, but as soon as the bed is continually dry they can be worn.

Hassle-free living with kids...
In Families

(see also **DEVELOPMENT, ON OUTINGS** *and* **AT WORK** *chapters)*

BABYSITTERS *(see* **ON OUTINGS** *chapter)*

COMMUNICATION

To encourage interaction amongst the members of your family, ask questions such as: What was the funniest thing that happened to you today? What was the happiest thing that happened to you today? What activity do you feel you achieved the best results in today?

To encourage your children to communicate with you:
— talk to your children about their ideas, plans, dreams and goals. Listen to them dream about being the 'Queen of England' without interrupting them to say that they need to be born into the royal family to be Queen. This may make them feel silly and reluctant to 'dream' with you again;

— never 'jump down their throats' when they come to tell you something. Even when you need to be firm and to discipline, try to always make them feel free to approach you;

— talk to your children about what you do at work. Don't lay all the burdens of work on them, but talk to them so they have a good idea of what you do during the day. All children know sometimes is that you have 'gone to work'!

— ask your children questions about their friends at school and kindergarten and about the things they do while they are there. If you do this in a friendly way, showing that you are interested in their world, they are more likely to come to you for advice and to discuss their problems;

— don't read the paper or watch television while your children are trying to talk with you about something. They need to know that what they have to say is important to you;

— even when you disagree with your children's point of view, always listen and show them that you are prepared to think about what they say.

FAMILY ACTIVITIES (see Family Nights, this chapter)

It is important for families to 'do' things together. Some suggestions: outings (see ON OUTINGS chapter); family jogging; exercising together; sports activities; gardening; hobbies; ice skating; musical activities; bush walking.

FAMILY RULES

Children often respond well to a set of rules. Make them as positive as possible, e.g. 'In our house, we have the television turned off while we are eating dinner' or 'In our family, we always telephone home if we want to play at our friends' places after school'. This should discourage children complaining about the fact that 'Mary is allowed to watch television while eating dinner in her house!'

FAMILY NIGHTS (see also ON OUTINGS chapter)

Special 'Family Nights' or days, can be some of the most special times in your children's lives and can be what the most precious childhood memories are made of. Whoever organises them doesn't necessarily have to spend too much time and energy doing so, but the more that goes into the night, the more everyone will get from it. The preparation time will be well worth it. Perhaps take it in turns to organise it, if you have some children old enough to do so. Low key family nights can be held once a week, with a really good one each month. Encourage every member of the family to keep that night free each week.

To increase the amount of time available to spend with the family:
— delegate household chores to every member of the family. They will be completed more quickly and a lot of interaction can take place while cleaning the house and doing dishes together;

— encourage your children to complete homework, music practice, household chores etc quickly so that there will be extra time to spend together playing games, going for walks, listening to music and so on.

Family Nights Ideas

Delegate a particular night (or day) as often as you can to be together and do things as a family. **Some suggestions:**
— have some nights as special colour nights, e.g. Black and White Night or Pink Night, when everyone dresses up in those colours, you eat food of those colours and use those colours as much as possible while you are talking. Of course, set the table with flowers, tablecloth and plates to coordinate, if possible. *(see* Family Night's Special Meals, *following);*

— arrange a family fashion show. You may want to carry it along the colour theme or it may have some other theme. The funniest are usually the most weird and wonderful colour themes, e.g. for a yellow fashion show you could have people dressing up in yellow beach towels with necklaces made from circles of corn kernels and so on;

— have a family Games night. Choose different games that are suitable for the different ages in the family;

— have a night where each member of the family can choose one short activity for everyone to join in with. A toddler may choose play dough, a seven-year-old may choose skipping, a thirteen-year-old may choose mathematics, father may choose reading the newspaper and mother may choose baking;

— tell the family that you will be celebrating something, but keep it a secret, until the night. The family could perhaps try to guess what they are celebrating and make up 'Congratulations' cards for things like the cat's birthday, one more year to go before starting school, seven years since Hannah cut her first tooth and so on.

Family Night's Special Meals

In order to make the most of the time available on 'Family Nights', consider using paper plates for dinner, which can be thrown away instead of washed.

Use your imagination to add fun and variety to a Family Meal Time:
— when someone asks you 'What is for dinner?', make up some crazy reply like 'elephant trunks and tomato sauce', or 'mud pies and wood chips';

— everyone could pretend to be someone else in the family and, while eating, a four-year-old could talk about her day as daddy at work, father could talk about his day at home as mother, mother could be baby etc;

— take your dinner outside and have a picnic under the stars or, on a wet night, eat your dinner on your veranda and look at the rain.

Family Story Times

— use a family photograph album. Each person can have a turn at telling the story of what happened on that occasion. This is especially enjoyable after a holiday;

— tell the children stories about your childhood. Choose as many funny ones as possible to get everybody laughing;

— have grandparents and older members of the family tell stories about 'the olden days!';

— play a game where each person has a turn to mime something funny that has happened in the family recently. The children will enjoy being able to make fun of 'mum when she got her foot stuck in the mud', for example.

FATHERS

Fathers can greatly help their wives, who are new mothers, to feel a bit more human at times by:
— arriving home from work when expected. Dinner time is usually the most exhausting and an extra few minutes alone with the children can be difficult to handle at times;

— arriving home in a good mood. Men need time to unwind after a busy day, so try to relax as much as possible on your way home, rather than collapsing in a heap on the lounge chair when you arrive. Your children need time to be with you and talk with you before going to bed;

— if baby is very unsettled when you arrive home, consider taking her for a walk by yourself, so that mother can relax. It will help you to relax as well;

— arrange to have a take-away meal every so often;

— plan to take your wife out occasionally so that she can enjoy some adult company;

— even if all she has to talk about is the baby's crying, make a real effort to listen to your wife, who could be starving for an adult's listening ear

FIGHTING

To discourage criticism and complaining in children:
— counteract any unnecessary criticism with kind words;

— give each child a small supply of 'complaint tickets'. Each time they want to make a complaint they have to forfeit a ticket. This should help them to think twice before complaining unnecessarily;

— make a rule 'No fighting at the meal table';

— avoid competitive play and games with children who tend to fight a lot;

— encourage co-operative play.

If fighting amongst siblings is a problem in the family, make up a 'Friendly Chart' for each child with a column for each day. Mark a cross when a child lapses into fighting or arguing and reward a clear column at the end of each day with a sticker or a star. Decide how many stars would warrant a greater prize at the end of the week or how many crosses would deserve a cancellation of pocket money, television viewing or some other suitable deterrent. Instead of having to reprimand all the time, let the children see you walking to the chart and hopefully they will abandon their squabble.

To put an end to a bad squabble amongst your children:
— offer to read the children a story or play a game with them;

— take the children for a walk and distract them by talking about things observed along the way;

— ask the children involved if they can come up with a solution to the problem. If, for example, they are fighting over who will sit next to the dog in the car, with a little guidance, they may come up with the idea that one person sits next to the dog on the way there and the other on the way back.

MEMENTOS (see Photographs, this chapter)

Parents, keep a record of your child's language development. Get started now and write down:
— when they said their first words;

— their vocabulary at various times in their first two years or so;

— funny words they used for different things;

— amusing things they said.

Keep a cassette tape for each child, recording their first sounds and cries, their gurgling noises, their first words, laughter, talking, playing, songs etc. A good time to record is when they are in the bath, playing with their toys.

Keep pieces of your children's hair, at different stages, to show the difference in colour and texture.

Keep one or two of your children's first teeth as a memento of their early childhood.

Other mementos of your children's early years could include: hospital name tags; baby clinic record book; your diary of baby's first year; baby's first letter; hand and foot prints; baby's first drawing and painting; height chart.

Make up a recipe book over the years of your children's favourite recipes, to give to them when they leave home.

MOTHERS

Be Prepared (see Planning, this chapter, Nappy Bags in AND THEIR CLOTHES and Be Prepared in ON OUTINGS chapter)

To make it easier to handle the early morning rush, get into the habit of preparing things the night before, e.g. pack baby's bag, make the school lunches, lay out the clothes for the children for the following day, set the breakfast table etc.

Breastfeeding

If you have older children at home, make sure you have them organised before you start to breastfeed:

— check to see that they are playing in a safe place. They may like to sit down near you with some puzzles or a taped story;

— have a drink or your child's meal ready for her to eat nearby at the same time;

— if the older child uses a potty, have that handy or try to get an older child to use the toilet first. It is amazing how these sudden needs arise, while attending to baby!;

— use the time while feeding to cuddle up with your toddler, to read him a story;

— bring the child's teddy or doll with you so that she can look after it. Suggesting that they play with their dolls may often give a negative response, but if you start playing with it, the child will often want to take over;

— take the telephone off the hook, if you can't reach it while feeding.

To make yourself feel better when having to feed in the middle of the night, keep a flask of your favourite hot drink, or cold in summer, ready for when you wake up. Be very careful, in your semi-conscious state, not to burn baby.

Cooking

If you have a busy schedule, save time by:
— planning the meals for the whole week and cooking twice as much of some foods as required and then using them the next day in a different way;

— regularly cooking in bulk;

— preparing dinner in the morning when baby is asleep or at the least busy time of the day.

Efficiency *(see* **Planning,** *this chapter)*

To give yourself more time and energy through the day:
— try getting up ten or fifteen minutes earlier, to put you ahead right at the beginning (try not to be tempted to count the number of hours you 'haven't slept' as that may make you feel tired just thinking about it!)

— start the day with a good breakfast to help eliminate fatigue in the middle of the morning.

Housework

To help you through the chores that you least enjoy:
— time yourself when doing these jobs. Next time try to beat your record. You might as well spend as little time as possible doing the tasks you don't like;

— play some stimulating music while you are working. Floors may get mopped in half the time if accompanied by the Minute Waltz or some up-tempo music;

— suggest to a friend or neighbour that you share household chores. You could help her clean out her pantry one week and she can help you the next. When it comes to cleaning windows, you will probably be very thankful;

— do your ironing with a neighbour. You will enjoy being able to talk while you work and your children may be able to play together at the same time;

— delegate work to other members of the family *(see* AT WORK *chapter).*

Don't get into bondage to the cliche, 'If a job is worth doing, it is worth doing well'. Sometimes a mother's time schedule doesn't allow a thorough job and usually a 'quick wipe' is better than no wipe at all.

Ironing *(see also* Ironing *in* AT WORK *chapter)*

To prevent a baby interfering with the iron and ironing board, your sewing bits and pieces, art work, painting project or your work on the computer, place the playpen around you whilst you are at work. This will give baby a lot more freedom without danger.

Looking After Yourself

Mothers are often the last to be attended to. Don't neglect yourself, as the whole family is counting on you. Eat well, exercise well and rest well. Remember that if you break down, there are no spare parts or replacements and contrary to popular thought, mothers do not come with a full guarantee!

When making sandwiches for your family's lunches, make some for yourself. Pack them up so they are ready for you to eat at any time.

Consider taking your packed lunch outside or down to the park for half an hour, **for a restful change of scenery.**

To help yourself to feel better:
— endeavour to get out of the house every day, preferably going for a walk with baby or children;

— try to arrange with a friend or neighbour to exchange some babysitting time so that you can go out or rest. You could look after her child one afternoon and vice versa;

— have some of your favourite music playing around the house;

— treat yourself to a perm or a facial. Looking good will help you to feel good.

Planning *(see* Be Prepared, *this chapter)*

To plan your day efficiently, make a list for each day of what you have to do, in order of priority. It is very satisfying to cross off each task as it is completed, before moving on to the next one. When you have a list of all that is required, it is also easier to organise your time and perhaps do a couple of things at the same time.

When you have a 'bored' pre-schooler at home, who seems to need your companionship through all her waking hours, prepare one or two exciting activities at night before you go to bed, for her to enjoy the next day. It can be difficult organising a painting or collage activity or making play dough while she is around and consequently they often get left undone. If you can set out everything for a particular activity, all ready to go, you will probably find your little one will play well alone for much longer.

To plan your week efficiently, try to organise 'In Days' and 'Out Days', if you don't go out to work. Where possible, keep 'In Days' for housework, sewing, painting and anything that requires you to be at home. Visiting, shopping and doctor's appointments can be organised for 'Out Days'. Of course, you will not always be able to keep to this, especially if you don't have much time to work around children's sleeps, but when you can, you will save a lot of time.

In order to be able to organise the family around its commitments, have a calendar, large enough to note the activities of every person in the family. Older children should be responsible for writing their engagements on the appropriate dates.

Preparing for a New Baby *(see also* Sibling Rivalry, *this chapter)*

To make it easier to cope with everything when you have a new baby:
— for several weeks before baby is due, every time you cook casseroles or bake, double or treble the quantities to keep in the freezer for later on when your time will be taken up;

— freeze extra sandwiches for your husband's or wife's or children's lunches.

Relaxation

It is important for mothers to have some form of relaxation. Some suggestions:
— take a few minutes to telephone a friend. Speaking with an adult will give you a boost!

— at lunch time, sit down with your cup of tea and listen to some quiet, relaxing music;

— take your children to the park to let off steam, while you relax under a tree, while supervising.

Sewing

If you are trying to sew while you have a toddler or baby around you, place a wooden play pen around you and the sewing machine so baby can't get into difficulty with the pins, the sewing machine and scissors. This will leave him free to play nearby without losing sight of mummy.

There are lots of activities children can do while you are sewing. *(See* Sewing *in* AT PLAY *chapter).*

Sickness

Contrary to popular opinion, mothers can get sick themselves! **If you are confined to bed while looking after a toddler:**
— have someone bring a supply of suitable toys and activities to the bedside, preferably on a table that you can easily reach;

— protect yourself from squirming children on the bed, by placing pillows or a cardboard box around or over any painful or vulnerable area of your body;

— set up a high chair or small table and chair for your little one to sit at while playing, so that he is not continually smothering you.

Talking on the Telephone

Children have an amazing ability to turn on tears and troubles while you are on the telephone. If you are on an important call, be armed with some things to distract your toddler from his great 'need' of your full attention:
— give him a clean feather to play with;

— hand out little pieces of sticky tape, one at a time;

— give him a toy telephone or an unused real telephone to speak into;

— let him use a stapler and some paper;

— give him his lunch or a snack;

— give him a handbag full of all sorts of safe and interesting bits and pieces;

— place head phones on his head with music or a story to listen to. If you have more than one child, play the music through the speakers as well so the second one doesn't feel left out.

MOVING HOUSE

Small children, in particular, can be adversely affected by changes in their environment and routines. These changes, along with the loss of familiar faces around them, can create considerable stress in children, especially if they are not well prepared for the transitions or if they sense stress in their parents.

To reduce stress in young children while moving house and to help your children feel at home, as quickly as possible, in their new house:
— make sure any 'cuddly' toy or blanket, that your child is especially attached to, is kept with you all the time and not packed away;

— keep all the child's familiar items, such as potty, feeding bowls and spoons, bedding, special toys etc with the child so that substitutes don't need to be used if they can't be found immediately;

— wherever possible, ensure that your child's feeding and sleeping times are kept to his normal routine;

— if possible, have their furniture put on the moving van last so it will be the first off the truck and in the new home, when it arrives;

— don't choose this time to introduce a new procedure to your little one. Wait until they are well settled in their new environment to begin toilet training, reducing day time sleeps, weaning, starting kindergarten etc;

— if possible allow your child to choose (or think she is choosing) which room she wants to sleep in or what colour she would like any necessary redecorating to be done in. The way you word the questions and gently guide his choices can often bring them around to giving you the answers that are most suitable!

To make moving house as little traumatic as possible for small children:
— if possible take them to see the new house before moving in;

— find something about the new house or area that will be exciting for the children and chat enthusiastically about it, e.g. children their own age in the street, planning picnics under the big tree etc;

— give your children a small suitcase or box, with their name on it, to pack some of their own special belongings in. At the new house, allow the child to unpack his own box and place these few things where he would like to keep them. This allows the child to think that he has assisted in the removal and he is assured that his special treasures have definitely been packed;

— be careful not to throw out any of your children's precious possessions which will be missed later on, as this could contribute to feelings of insecurity;

— if your children are not going to be around at the time of the shift, make sure they know exactly what to expect, such as where they are going, when they will be picked up etc, so that unnecessary fears will not develop;

— if possible take the family pet with you when you move.

PHOTOGRAPHS
(see **Family Time,** this chapter and **Books** in **AT PLAY** chapter)

Displaying Photographs

To display photographs, pin them to a large notice board in the family room. Visitors will enjoy looking at them and it will be fascinating to see how your family changes.

Make a photographic 'Family Tree'. Use duplicates, or photographs that are not too precious, and make it a family project. Use a large piece of card to stick the photographs on and felt pens to write the appropriate names and relationship. This is a good way to teach your children how they are related to their greater family.

Duplicate Photographs

When you order duplicate photographs, use the spare ones:
— to send as postcards, with a greeting written on the back;

— for the children's albums;

— to make into jigsaw puzzles.

Make up a photograph album for each child in the family. Label the albums with the person's name and date, e.g. Susan, February 1990 - March 1991.

Toddlers love looking at photographs of familiar people and places. Keep some photos in a cheap album, with clear plastic sleeves, for your young children to look at. If you normally use a more expensive album which is not quite as 'baby-proof', select a few photos that aren't too precious to put in a cheap album.

Labelling Photographs

To help you remember when photographs were taken, write down in your diary, on the calendar or on a list on your refrigerator, the dates of when you take photos. This will enable you to label them correctly.

Make a point of labelling the backs of photographs, as soon as you have them printed, with the date and age of the child and the setting.

If you don't put the photos in an album straight away, label the outside of each packet with the dates of the first and last photos and a general description, such as 'Christmas 1990', to make it easier to find them when you want them.

Negatives

Keep negatives in an envelope, glued inside the back of the photograph album in which the prints are displayed. The negatives will be easy to find and will store well.

Store negatives in a dry place, away from direct light.

If you have packets of negatives, after putting photographs in an album, write on the outside of the packet what the negatives are of.

Photographing Children

When photographing children, consider the following points:
— always keep your camera loaded and handy. The best shots of children are often the most spontaneous ones, when you least expect them;

— preferably choose an overcast day so that your subjects won't be in brilliant sunshine or heavy shade. The shade around the eyes or over the face can spoil good photos;

— if possible, avoid situations where the subjects are looking into the sun, as the result will usually be screwed up eyes and unhappy children;

— concentrate on capturing them being themselves! A zoom or telephoto lens will be very helpful.

To keep a good photographic record of a newborn baby's growth and progress, photograph her regularly, perhaps every week or two. It will be easier to compare them if you photograph them in the same spot each time, alongside the same prop, doing their latest trick! Label the photos with the dates and ages.

If you are trying to photograph a young child on your own, consider using some of the following props to make him smile:
— tie a colourful balloon to your head;

— place some sticky tape on the palms of a baby who is able to sit up. You should be able to capture some great expressions while he is investigating and trying to remove it;

— have a range of funny hats to put on;

— use a puppet to say funny things to the child;

— play 'peek-a-boo' from behind a door.

School Photographs

Display school photographs for the current year in a frame on the wall. Buy just one frame for each child and when the next school photo arrives, place it in front of the old one in the frame. It is a good way of storing them and one frame will hold quite a few photos.

When you get your school photographs write the names of each child in the class, as they appear, on the back of the photo. Your child may think she will never forget who they are, but in years to come she may appreciate being reminded of who her 'boyfriend' was in her first year at school.

Slides

Store photographic slides upright under specific headings in the long, thin cardboard boxes that plastic wrap and aluminium foil come in.

An occasional 'old fashioned slide show' can still bring much delight, especially when children can see themselves as a baby, enlarged on the wall. Select a few of the best prints of each child and use the negatives to get slides taken off. Not as many people choose slide film now, but it is possible to have both off the one negative.

SELF-ESTEEM (see also Sibling Rivalry, following)

To help each child feel that they are an important member of the family, try to share some uninterrupted time daily with each individual, doing something with the child, not just for the child.

To help raise your child's self-esteem:
— display to your child your own healthy sense of self-respect and self-esteem. Don't let her hear you putting yourself down;

— don't be defeatist in your conversation. Instead of saying 'I wouldn't be very good at that' or 'I'm too old...', why not say 'Let's give it a go' or 'that would be an interesting thing to try';

— when disciplining a child, talk about the unacceptable behaviour rather than calling the child 'bad' or 'naughty'. If you tell a child that he is 'bad' often enough, he will believe that you expect him to be naughty and will probably live up to your expectations;

— discourage any 'put-down' talk in your children, both about themselves or other people. People with a healthy self-esteem don't need to be threatened by others;

— encourage children to feel happy inside with their efforts when they work hard, rather than always having to rely on receiving material rewards for their achievements. Not everybody can win first prize, but everyone is entitled to feel satisfied when they know they have performed well;

— encourage children to look after their appearance. People will often feel much better about themselves if they feel that they look good;

— encourage children to become independent;

— encourage children to find their own forms of entertainment and pleasure. They should not be continually depending on television or other people for entertainment. Encourage them to 'have a go' at all sorts of different activities;

— encourage children to be able to laugh at themselves. Show them how you can laugh about some of your mistakes. This is one of the best ways of reducing the negative impact in a stressful situation.

Avoid embarrassing your children in front of others:
— try not to have to discipline your children in front of people. If possible, take them aside to save too much embarrassment on their part;

— be very careful not to compare one child with another;

— don't, without her consent, ask her to read out loud or perform in front of others;

— don't talk about him to others in a way that he would find embarrassing.

SIBLING RIVALRY *(see also* **Self-Esteem,** *prior entry)*
Preparing for Baby
To prepare a small child for the arrival of a new baby:
— make sure **you** tell the older child about the new baby so that he does not find out from someone else;

— always talk about the baby as 'our baby';

— talk about how pleased you felt when you were expecting him or her, and how exciting it was finding out whether you had a boy or girl;

— if possible, take them to visit a friend with a new baby and preferably let them see the baby being breastfed, if you intend breastfeeding your baby. It can come as a bit of a surprise for some children, to see their mothers feeding a baby;

— let them help you to sort out and choose clothes and toys and to decide where the baby will sleep and so on;

— you could take her for an outing to look at the hospital where baby will be born;

— make sure your children realise that the new baby will not be an 'instant playmate' or you could find that they feel really disappointed with a 'useless' baby who only seems to cry all the time. Talk to them about how she will develop and that after quite a long while they will be able to play together;

— if the older child is to stay with someone else when the baby is born, try to arrange for her to stay there beforehand;

— get the children to help organise a 'Welcome Home' for mother and baby;

— try to make it possible for the older child to be there when the baby arrives home from hospital so that he doesn't feel that an intruder has taken over 'his' home while he was away.

If the older child is about ready to change from the cot to a bed, make the change well before baby arrives so that it doesn't seem like she has to vacate 'her' cot for the baby. If possible, put the cot into storage for a while so that the older child will start to forget about it. It can be a good idea to change the cot a little for baby, perhaps with a coat of paint or a couple of transfers.

Visits to the Hospital

If your older child is likely to get upset when having to leave the hospital after visits, give her little inexpensive gifts or secret messages in envelopes to be opened when she gets into the car.

When an older child is first taken up to the hospital to visit:
— try to arrange for the baby to be in the bassinet or in the nursery when the older child first comes to the hospital for a visit, rather than in mother's arms. A young child will not automatically understand that you have enough love for two children and she could well feel displaced!

— give the older child a little present 'from the baby' and some little treats from mother too;

— consider giving the child a colouring-in book or some other activity book which he can bring up to show you his progress in, each time he visits. This will give him a special project to work on at home and something to show off to mum;

— be prepared to have to give the child a snack, if she can see patients eating or drinking. Many 'tantrums' are sparked off in hospitals when toddlers see food that they can't have. If visiting around a meal time, perhaps arrange to have his sandwiches brought up to the hospital.

Coming Home from Hospital

When bringing baby home from hospital:
— consider taking your older child into the hospital too and perhaps giving her a 'baby doll' to bring home from the hospital, preferably one that can be bathed;

— if your older children are at home when mother and baby return, have someone else carry the baby so that mother's arms are free to cuddle her older children.

Jealousy *(see* Breastfeeding *in* Mothers *section, this chapter)*

In order to keep jealousy to a minimum, when a new baby arrives in the family:
— let the older child introduce the baby to people;

— if possible, allow the child to help feed and bath the baby;

— try to satisfy her requests to hold the baby, with you close by, of course. A toddler is almost as likely to drop a baby when she has 'finished with it', as she is a toy! Teach her how to gently stroke the baby with the palms of her hands, rather than her fingers and to tell you when she has had enough;

— spend as much time as possible alone with the older child each day;

— at times, when the baby is crying, let your older children hear you say to the baby 'you will just have to wait for a few minutes while I get lunch for James and Sarah'. This will reinforce, to the older children, the truth that they are just as important as the baby;

— try not to make too many changes for the older child at the same time, e.g. choose another time to potty train them or to change their bedroom or to start them at kindergarten, if possible;

— this time could be used to introduce a special privilege, so she can see that there are advantages in being older. Perhaps she could be given a new pet, to help to look after, or it may be a fitting time to start introducing some pocket money.

When people come bearing gifts for baby:
— allow your older child to open them if she wants to;

— have a small wrapped gift handy, just in case there are problems.

To discourage feelings in a child that baby can do no wrong while she can do no right!
— try not to be always reprimanding the older child for being rough with the baby. Of course they can be dangerous in their 'affections' for their new 'doll', but keep negatives to a minimum. Now is the time to be as creative as possible in thinking up all the distractions you can use. When you see two index fingers aiming for two eyes, try saying something like 'feel his little toes, aren't they funny little things. What do you think they look like? You had toes just like that when you were a little baby'. Rather than saying 'Don't poke his nose' all the time, try to rephrase it so the child doesn't always feel like the loser, e.g. 'We don't poke baby's face, because we don't want to hurt him.'

The most important thing that your older children will require when a baby is in the house, is your time. If necessary, leave some of the housework so that you can make time to spend, just with them. Get really involved in what they are doing, by jumping into the sandpit with them or crawling around the floor, playing with their cars. A child will always feel more important when an adult is prepared to get down to their level. Being able to look right into your face is much more satisfying than having to look at your knee caps all the time!

SPECIAL TIME (see Self-Esteem and Sibling Rivalry, this chapter)

If you sense that one of your children particularly needs some quality time alone with you, consider having a 'spa' together. You don't need to have a spa bath, but you could call it a spa. You may decide to wear bathing suits and in winter it would be a lovely warm treat, while in summer a cool and refreshing time to be together, talking, playing and appreciating each other. This could also be a reward for some particularly special effort on the part of a child.

TELEVISION

To help guard against your children's indiscriminate viewing of television:
— if possible, video-tape the programmes that you are happy for your children to watch. This way, they will be available for your children to see at times suitable to you, rather than when the television programmers dictate. Young children enjoy repetition and so will not mind seeing the same 'Sesame Street' and 'Muppet Show' programmes many times, which means you will not need to replace the tapes too often;

— use a television guide to plan ahead the programmes that your children may watch;

— supervise television viewing and be ready to turn it off as soon as something comes on that is violent, frightening or promoting values beneath your own;

— decide which days have the very best family programmes and make the others 'Television Off Days';

— get the whole family into the habit of turning the television off as soon as the particular programme they are watching is finished. If you don't turn it off straight away, something else that 'looks interesting' can lure an undisciplined viewer;

— discuss the programmes that you watch, to ensure that your children gain maximum benefit from them;

— get your children interested in sports, reading, outdoor play, hobbies, music and other activities whose value will usually surpass that of constant television viewing.

TRADITIONS
(see **Christmas Traditions** in **ON SPECIAL OCCASIONS** chapter)

WHEN DADDY OR MUMMY GOES AWAY

To keep daddy's or mummy's voice in the home while he or she is away, have him or her record stories to be played to the children at bed time. Some stories can be played while the little ones are following the pictures in the book. Ring a bell or tell them on the tape when it is time to turn the pages.

To help your preschooler remember all the interesting things that have happened while daddy or mummy was away, have her collect little keepsakes in a special box. A shell will remind her to tell daddy or mummy what happened when she went to the beach, a bus ticket will remind her about her trip to town and a little bit of sand in a matchbox will remind her to tell daddy or mummy about what she built in the sandpit at kindergarten.

HASSLE-FREE LIVING WITH KIDS:...
Grooming

(see also IN THE BATHROOM)

APPEARANCE

To encourage children to take care of their appearance, have a mirror on the wall in the bathroom at their height. This will help them to brush their hair and clean their teeth more thoroughly. Mirror tiles can be bought quite cheaply.

FINGERNAILS

To cut a baby's or child's fingernails more easily:

— sit baby on your lap, facing forward, so that his nails are in the same position as yours are when you are cutting them;

— use blunt-ended scissors;

— cut them after a bath, when they are soft and clean;

— put talcum powder in your hands and gently draw baby's fingers through it so that his nails fill with powder. This will make the nails easier to see;

— cut them while the child is distracted by a story or television;

— wait until she is asleep so she won't wriggle around too much and cut them or gently rip them with your teeth.

GLASSES

If your child's glasses slip down on her nose, glue two small pieces of rubber, which have been cut from a large, flat rubber band, on to the inside of the nose piece.

HAIR ACCESSORIES
Hair Bands

To keep elastic hair bands handy:
— place them around the door knobs in the rooms you are most likely to need them;

— twist them around the handle of your hair brush;

Hair Clips

To keep fancy hair clips in place, glue a thin, narrow strip of plastic foam to the back of the hair clip.

To keep fancy hair clips tidy, hang a piece of ribbon on your daughter's bedroom wall and simply fasten the hair clips to it when they are not being worn. If the colour fits in with the decor, the ribbon will look quite attractive.

To make inexpensive, fancy hair clips for children, attach a decorative button, such as an animal or flower, to a normal hair pin. The button will need to have quite a large eyelet.

Hair Ribbons

To keep hair ribbons neat, hang them from a large, plastic bulldog clip on a hook.

HAIR CUTTING

To keep a child 'hair free' during a haircutting session:
— supply a plastic raincoat to wear;

— slip an old half-slip petticoat, with the elastic tightened a little, over their heads;

— cut a hole in the centre of a large, old towel and place this over the child's head.

To cut a child's fringe straight, place a piece of clear sticky tape on the hair along the cutting line and use it as a guide. Preferably put the tape on the part that will be cut off to avoid having to remove it from the hair.

HAIR WASHING

To wash a baby's hair easily, hold him under your arm, with his head in your hand, under the kitchen tap or any other mixer tap you have. You only need one arm to hold baby and the other is free to wash his hair, without getting water on his face.

To keep water and shampoo out of your children's eyes at hair-washing time:
— dab a little petroleum jelly or cold cream over the eyebrows and eyelids;

— let them wear swimming goggles.

To keep children's neck and shoulders dry while their hair is being washed:
— make an old towel into a cape. Cut a hole in the middle of the towel, large enough to go over the child's head. To make it even more effective, hem the edge of the hole and insert elastic through the round hem.

— get them to wear an old nylon raincoat.

To make hair washing time more enjoyable, place a mirror in a position so the child can easily see herself and have fun together making different shapes with the soapy hair. Try making a crown, goat horns and crazy hair styles.

When washing children's hair in the bath, rinse out the last of the shampoo in the hair with a jug of warm water to which has been added a tablespoon of vinegar. This will help to get rid of the soap and help it to shine.

When your children start washing their own hair, prevent wastage by measuring out the amount of shampoo they should use and leaving it in a plastic lid or other suitable container for them.

To remove knots and tangles from a child's hair, fill a plastic spray bottle with water and hair conditioner. Spray the knots before gently brushing.

To remove chewing gum from hair, try one of the following:
— massage some unbeaten egg white into the hair;

— rub it with an ice cube to freeze the gum and then peel it off;

— massage some peanut butter or cold cream into the chewing gum to loosen it from the hair and then remove with a paper towel. Shampoo hair;

— rub the chewing gum with some cooking oil on a piece of cotton wool.

JEWELLERY
Pierced Earrings

To prevent irritations to the skin caused by poor-quality metal, clean the earring with methylated spirits and then paint over the bar and butterfly clip with two thin coats of clear nail polish. The backs of clip-on earrings can also be treated this way.

If your children's pierced ears become sore or inflamed, dip the pointed end of the earring into an antiseptic ointment before poking it through the ear.

To keep earrings neatly stored:
— press earrings for pierced ears through small holes in a piece of cardboard, foam plastic or heavy plastic;

— keep them in separate compartments of an egg carton.

Storing Jewellery

Keep children's jewellery in empty egg cartons. Matching items can be sorted into separate compartments.

A doll makes a great jewellery holder. Hang bracelets over the doll's wrists, necklaces over her head, rings on out-stretched fingers and earrings clipped on to her dress or apron.

Watches

To clean white plastic watch straps, scrub them with toothpaste on an old, firm toothbrush.

To prevent the face of your child's watch scratching, cover it with clear, self-adhesive plastic.

TEETH
Accidents With Teeth

To try to save one of your children's second teeth that has been knocked out:
— act quickly. If the tooth is replaced within about half an hour,

the chances of success are much higher.

— holding the tooth by the crown, not the root, rinse in saliva or tepid milk, to clean off any dirt. Rinse in water only as a last resort;

— replace the tooth straight away in the mouth if possible and go immediately to a dentist;

— if the patient is hurt too much or for some reason you cannot replace the tooth, take it to the dentist in a container of milk, in a wet handkerchief or sitting in the saliva, next to the gum in the child's mouth.

Cleaning Teeth

Start cleaning baby's gums before the first tooth has broken through. Place a soft, damp piece of muslin cloth on your finger and rub it around the gums regularly to clean them.

Before you start to clean your baby's teeth:
— run your clean finger around his gums a few times, before introducing a toothbrush, to get him used to the sensation;

— test his reaction to the flavour of the toothpaste by placing a little on your finger and letting him suck it. If he really detests the flavour, try another flavour or brush his teeth without any paste on the brush initially, to get him used to the procedure. It is important not to let him be put off the whole business simply because he doesn't like the flavour of the toothpaste, as it may take a long time for him to cooperate again.

— let him see you cleaning your teeth frequently. No doubt he will want to 'have a go'.

If your child does not want to cooperate when you are trying to clean her teeth, give her your toothbrush and open your mouth for her to clean your teeth. While she is busy, clean her teeth!

To make sure small children clean their teeth, line up their toothbrushes with toothpaste on them, by the bathroom basin each morning and night. You will probably also save on toothpaste!

Because young children find it difficult to brush their own teeth correctly, an adult should thoroughly brush the teeth of children younger than about eight years old, at least once every day. Stand behind him, tilting his head back enough for you to be able to see clearly into his mouth.

Teething (see DEVELOPMENT chapter)

Toothbrushes

To freshen a toothbrush and keep it hygienic:
— don't leave your toothbrush sitting, head-down in a tumbler. Stand it upright so the bristles can dry out;

— always rinse out all the left-over toothpaste from your brush, after use;

— soak it for several hours in a mild solution of salt and water;

— soak it in a bottle-sterilising solution.

Tooth Decay

To help avoid tooth decay in small children, don't allow them to go to bed after drinking milk or fruit juice or eating dried fruit (or sweets, of course), without cleaning their teeth. Dates and sultanas etc have a very high sugar content and the small pieces which get embedded in the crevices of the back teeth can easily cause decay. Milk also has sugar in it. Only give water to drink after the teeth have been cleaned.

If your children cannot survive without sweets, allow them to eat them after a meal and just before cleaning their teeth. It is not a good idea to spread the 'nibbling' out during the day as this only allows the sugar to be in the mouth for a longer period, thus encouraging decay.

Always clean your child's teeth after giving medicines, which are usually contained in sugary syrups.

HASSLE-FREE LIVING WITH KIDS...
On holiday

(see also **IN TRANSIT***)*

BEACH
Baby at the Beach

To prevent a baby's food getting covered with sand, take along an inflatable paddling pool to the beach. Inflate the pool, line the bottom with an old clean sheet or tablecloth and sit baby in it at lunchtime or whenever food is given.

An inflatable paddling pool can also be used as a bed for baby to sleep in at the beach. Remember to take along a beach umbrella so you can be guaranteed that your baby can be in the shade. (All the shade under trees may be already occupied)!

Beach Toys *(see also* **Sand***, this chapter)*

Teach your children not to attempt to **retrieve a beach ball** that has floated out beyond the depth at which they are playing.

Crowded Beaches

To prevent children losing their parents or friends on a crowded beach:
— tie a few bright balloons or ribbons to the top of your beach umbrella or a large stick poked into the ground;
— dress your children in brightly coloured togs and sun hats so that you can easily identify them in the crowd.

Dressing Children

To make it easier to dress children after they have been swimming, take some talcum powder with you to the beach.

Drinks

To reduce the number of requests for drinks, give each person a plastic bottle with drink which has been frozen. As the ice melts, they will be able to drink a little more. (This is also a good idea for travelling in a car with children on a hot day. There will be fewer spills as well.)

Jewellery

To prevent children losing money, keys, watch or jewellery at the beach:
— sew a pocket onto a corner of their beach towel with a zip across the top;
— keep a clear capsule bottle in the beach bag to put them in. You will be able to see the time on the watch without getting sand in it;
— keep a large safety pin pinned to the inside lining of their beach bag. Keys and jewellery can be slipped on to the safety pin, which, if pinned to the bag, will not be able to slip into the sand and get lost.

Sand

To remove sand from a baby's eye, wash the eye with plenty of cold water, or put two drops of castor oil in the corner of the eye to help the sand float out.

To save carrying sand home with you:
— take an old paintbrush with you to brush the sand off shoes and toys, before leaving the beach;
— carry the beach toys in a plastic mesh bag or in a small plastic

laundry basket. When it is time to leave, dip the bag or basket full of toys in the water to wash off the sand.

Swimming At The Beach
(see also **Swimming** *in* **AT PLAY** *chapter)*

Make sure your children:
— swim between the flags at the beach;

— obey all signs and warnings at the beach;

— continually check their positions when swimming at the beach, as it is very easy to drift out of patrolled areas and into danger.

BED TIME

If you don't have a portable cot:
— take the playpen and a mattress with you to use as a cot while on holiday. It can be used as a safe playing area during the day, covered with a sheet if necessary for shade;

— a small baby can sleep in an inflated paddling pool. Use blankets, sheepskin or pillows for padding. Make sure the baby's face is not against the plastic;

— a small baby can sleep in an inflatable boat.

To help children (and adults) find their way to the toilet at night in a strange place, take along a night light to use at the motel or holiday house.

If you don't have a sleeping bag, use a large stitch to sew up the end and side flaps of a continental quilt. It will easily be able to be unpicked afterwards.

BELONGINGS

To save confusion, try to keep each child's bag, lunch box, drink bottle, plates, cups etc in the one colour so that everyone knows at a glance which is theirs.

To name children's plastic plates, mugs, torch etc, paint a strip of nail polish on to a cleaned part of the plastic and when it is half dry write the child's name with a pencil or sharp object.

To ensure that your children return with all their belongings from school and church camps, stick a list of all they are taking on the inside lid of their suitcases before they go. They will be able to check everything off as they pack to come home.

To help children identify their own luggage more easily, wrap something bright, such as a ribbon or piece of insulation tape around the handle.

CAMP FIRES

To save children burning themselves when cooking sausages or marshmallows on a fire, poke the stick through an aluminium pie plate before putting the sausage on it. If the plate is up near their hands, it will reflect the heat and stop them getting too hot.

In case you can't find suitable sticks for cooking sausages and marshmallows on, take along metal coathangers to use instead. The heat of the metal inside the sausage will help it to cook quickly too, but watch that they don't burn your hands.

Use metal skewers to cook baked potatoes on, on a camp fire. The heat of the metal will speed up the cooking time.

Children will enjoy blowing bubbles around the camp fire at night. The bubbles look great moving around in the hot air near the smoke and the flames. They can follow them with a torch too.

CAMPING (see also Tents and Tramping, this chapter)

When taking a torch away camping:
— use sticky tape to keep the switch on the off position, in case it is accidentally switched on in transit, with the movement of the articles in the bag;

— attach a strip of luminous tape to the torch or to matches and a candle so that they can be spotted in the dark.

To have everything ready for sleeping, when going on a camping trip, roll up pyjamas, toiletries and anything else required for the first night, in the sleeping bag. You will not have to unpack everything in the dark to find what is needed.

While showering at a camping ground, put your clothes, towels and toilet gear in a plastic supermarket bag to keep them dry, off the ground and together.

Keep a piece of foam plastic in the bottom of your child's soap container, when he goes camping. The sponge can be used as a washer and it will absorb any excess moisture in the container.

If you don't have any pegs while camping, use a piece of twisted twine or rope, attached at each end to the guy ropes of the tent or to trees. Pull the corners of the garments through the twists in the rope to hold them.

To make a portable clothes' line for camping, use an old umbrella which has had its cover taken off. Hang it upside down from its handle and peg the washing to the stays.

If you are taking a wooden playpen with you when you go camping, it can double as a clothes' line. Turn the playpen up on its side and hang the clothes over the rungs across the top and down the sides.

To keep toddlers safely within your campsite, make a fence from some lengths of scrim or shade cloth around the circumference of the area. Hold it up with a few stakes.

COOKING *(see also Camp Fires, this chapter)*

To save tired and hungry children getting upset while waiting for dinner when they arrive at their destination, prepare the first meal before leaving home so that it can be eaten as soon as you arrive, without having to unpack first.

OVERSEAS HOLIDAYS *(see Air Travel in IN TRANSIT chapter)*

When planning an overseas trip with children:
— try to involve the children in the planning by encouraging them to get brochures about the countries to be visited;

— read some books to the children about the countries so they have some idea of what they are likely to see;

— use a world globe to help your child understand where you are going;

— if visiting countries which use a foreign language, find a few simple words or phrases to teach your children before they arrive. They will enjoy speaking and being understood in a foreign language;

— remember to take out health insurance.

When travelling around in a foreign country with children:
— show your children what a policeman looks like, so they will know who to go to for help if they happen to get into difficulty;

— write the name of the child and the address and phone number of the place you are staying at on a piece of paper and pin it to the inside of the child's pocket or clothes.

PACKING FOR HOLIDAYS

When deciding what to take away on holiday for baby, write a list of everything you use for him from first thing in the morning until last thing at night and then go through the list, cutting out what is not necessary or putting in lighter, more portable substitutes where possible. Be prepared to have baby's luggage take up ninety percent of the available space!

When packing for a baby, use clear plastic bags to hold different items so that you will be able to tell at a glance, what is inside. This way you can keep all the bibs together, the plastic pants together, singlets, cardigans etc.

When children are travelling by themselves:
— pack the clothes for each day in separate plastic bags, labelled with the appropriate day. This will save her hunting for all the individual items. The dirty clothes can then be put back into the bag, before being put back into the suitcase. This should keep her case neat and functional;

— keep shoes, underwear, toilet gear etc separate in clear plastic bags. This will keep their bag neat and will enable them to see at a glance what they are looking for.

Keep children's swimming gear handy so you won't need to unpack everything before they can go for a swim.

When taking toddlers camping, take along their favourite push-along or ride-on toy. They will probably be able to amuse themselves for ages riding around the camping ground.

To remember what you should take with you on your next holiday, write a list of all the things you found useful this time and the things you wish you had taken on this holiday, when you get back from this holiday. Tape the list to the inside of your suitcase.

PICNICS

To make a tablecloth to use on picnics and barbecues:
— use an old shower curtain. Sew elastic around each corner, like a fitted sheet, so the wind won't blow it away. This cloth could also be used as an everyday cloth inside while the children are learning to feed themselves;

— use an old large towel. It is easy to wash and you can wipe your hands on it.

To keep your picnic food cool, freeze a large bottle of juice or cordial that you intend taking and place it in the cool box.

Keep a list of everything you need to take on a picnic, on the inside of your picnic hamper, so you won't forget anything. Children can pack the hamper by going through the list.

SUN

Children will find it easier to apply suntan lotion, when it is stored in a roll-on deodorant bottle. Take the plastic ball top out of the bottle and thoroughly wash and dry it. Fill the bottle, replace the lid and be sure to keep the cap tightly screwed on. Store upside down.

TENTS (see Camping, this chapter)

To stop people tripping over the guy ropes of a tent at night, paint some patches on the rope with fluorescent paint.

To make your tent easily identifiable in a large camping ground, attach a bright handkerchief, flag or ribbons to the top of the highest pole or to a nearby tree or car aerial.

TRAMPING AND WALKING (see also Walking in ON OUTINGS)

As a safety precaution when tramping, always take along the following:
— a whistle to blow in case you get lost (it is easier to blow a whistle over a long period of time than it is to shout);
— a waterproof package of matches (see Camping, this chapter);
— clothes warm enough to allow for a longer period outside than expected;
— strong walking shoes;
— some 'Scroggin' (a mixture of dried fruit, nuts and chocolate for energy).

When taking babies for walks in a front or back pack, have someone regularly check that the sun isn't glaring in their eyes or burning their skin. Keep a sunhat on them during the day.

WASHING (see Camping, this chapter)

To keep dirty clothes separate from clean ones, give children plastic bags to put their clothes in as soon as they are ready to be washed. This will keep their clean clothes fresh and it will make unpacking and washing easier at the end of their camp or holiday.

HASSLE-FREE LIVING WITH KIDS...
At meal times

BABY FOOD JARS

Use empty baby food jars for storing:

— home-made baby food in the freezer or refrigerator. Don't fill them quite to the top. If going out you can easily take one of the jars of frozen food, which will be thawed by the time you need it;

— spices, sesame seeds etc.

Before opening a can of baby food, wipe over the top with a clean, damp cloth to eliminate any possibility of contamination from the lid.

BARBECUES *(see* Training Cup *section of* Drinks, *this chapter)*

To make it easier to turn sausages on a barbecue, poke one metal skewer cross-wise right through the middle of all the sausages, before placing them on to cook. You will only need to turn the skewer once for all the sausages to be turned over.

If you wish to give children bread and salad at a barbecue, fill pita or pocket bread with the salad, to make it easier to eat, without too much mess.

If you are using a portable barbecue with children around, prevent burns by:
— placing it inside a play pen;
— if you have a fenced pool and the pool is not in use, place the barbecue within the safety of the childproof fence;
— if your back yard is fenced off from the front, place the barbecue in the front, with the gate shut, so small children will not be able to get near it.

BIBS *(see also* **Self-Feeding,** *this chapter and* **AND THEIR CLOTHES** *chapter)*

To catch spilled liquids:
— slip a piece of sponge rubber in the pocket of baby's plastic bib;
— use one of the hard plastic bibs with a permanent 'catcher' at the bottom.

To give better coverage and protection, safety-pin the bottom of a towelling bib to baby's clothes.

BOTTLES

To stop baby's bottles falling over in the refrigerator, stand them in a small cardboard crate that bottled drinks come in. You can easily lift out the bottles to get at other items in the fridge.

To remove the white chalky residue in a baby's bottle, boil it for ten minutes in a pan of water, to which has been added 1 cup white vinegar.

To remove any smell of sour milk from the baby's bottle, fill it with warm water and 1 teaspoon baking soda. Shake it well and leave it to soak for about 3 hours.

To keep the bottles, tops and teats together in the dishwasher, tie them up in a net bag with a drawstring.

To prevent accidents, make a rule that baby does not walk around with a bottle in his mouth. If he has a bottle, he must lie or sit in the one place until he has finished drinking.

To unclog the hole in a bottle's teat, use a plastic toothpick to gently push through the hole.

Before discarding the sterilising solution that you have sterilised bottles in, pour it into an ice cream container and soak dish cloths and brushes in it. Use it for anything else that needs a good clean.

To help wean a toddler off a bottle:
— put a straw in the bottle;

— take the top off the bottle and let your toddler drink from the bottle as if it were a cup;

— when the teat, that he is using now, wears out, let him put it in the rubbish bin. Tell him that it is no longer any good and so there is 'no more bottle';

— if you know a young baby who 'needs' his bottle, get him to give it to her as a present;

— if the child is getting older, but showing no signs of wanting to give up the bottle, allow a staged 'accident' to happen with the bottle, such as its melting in the dishwasher or breaking! Show the child what has happened to the bottle, saying that it is 'no good now and will have to be thrown away!'

BREAKFAST

To keep a toddler happy while he is waiting for his breakfast, sit him in the highchair with a few pieces of dry breakfast cereal to nibble on. Make sure he doesn't choke and that the cereal is not coated in sugar or food colouring.

BREASTFEEDING *(see also* Mothers *and* Sibling Rivalry *in* IN FAMILIES *chapter and* Feeding Babies, *this chapter)*

To express milk when you have sore or cracked nipples, fill a large, clean jar with boiling water and leave it for ten minutes. Empty the jar and smear petroleum jelly around the top. Place the mouth of the jar on the breast around the nipple. The vacuum caused by the cooling air inside the jar will gently draw milk out.

If you tend to forget which breast you fed from last, attach a small safety pin to your bra strap on the side you last fed from. Swap it from side to side after each feed.

CHILDREN IN THE KITCHEN

To encourage toddlers to become helpful and independent in the kitchen, keep their plastic cups, bowls and plates in a low cupboard or drawer, which they can reach. When preparing snacks, ask them to help you get their own utensils.

DRINKING

To help a small child grip a glass to drink from, place a few rubber bands around the glass at regular intervals. Preferably use plastic tumblers for small children.

To discourage a child from habitually asking for a drink after he or she has been put to bed, leave a plastic bottle with a little fresh water in it and a plastic mug beside the bed. If you have a plastic bottle or cup with its own straw in the top, that will be even better.

When first giving drinks to your babies, give water, so they become used to drinking it. If you do start giving them juice, make it extremely diluted so they will not get used to drinking very sweet drinks. Use about as much fruit juice as you would use cordial. This will be more economical and far better for them. Fruit juices that are very concentrated can lead to food allergies.

If your child is used to drinking sweet drinks, wean her off them gradually, by diluting them more and more or reducing the sugar content gradually.

To encourage children to drink water instead of fruit juice or cordial all the time, tell them that they can have a glass of juice (well-diluted) after they have drunk a glass of water. Do this also with milk and flavoured milk.

To encourage a child to drink plenty of water:
— in summer, place different shaped ice cubes in the drink, or ice cubes containing tiny pieces of fruit in them;

— allow him to use a straw to drink the water with.

To stop drinks being knocked off the table or highchair tray, draw a circle on the tray or place a round piece of paper or plastic in the safest position for the cup to be placed. Have your child always put his drink on its 'house' in between sips.

Straws

Teach baby to drink with a straw at a young age. It is easiest to do this while they still have the sucking reflex, at around six months. Then as they get older, you won't have to worry about not having a feeding cup when you go out as baby will be able to drink from a straw. Shop assistants are usually quite happy to give you a glass of water and a straw for little children.

To teach a young child to drink from a straw, use a bendy straw or one that is not too long to manage. Dip the 'sucking end' into a drink that you know he enjoys and then put it in the child's mouth. He will probably want to suck to get more of it.

To make it easier for young children to drink from fruit juice boxes, insert a long, flexible straw instead of the short straws which come with the juice. It is more difficult for the juice to squirt out of a long straw. It is preferable, however, to give fruit juice to children only when it is well diluted. The sugar content in juice is high and can encourage a 'sweet tooth'.

To prevent a child spilling a drink when using a long straw, cut the straw down to the appropriate size for the glass that she is drinking from.

Training Cups

To clean the lids of trainer cups, soak them for several hours in a bottle-sterilising solution. This should remove germs, stains and food particles from the spouts. Rinse thoroughly.

Keep your toddler's training cup, when he is finished with it:
— for your children to use while travelling in the car;

— to use as a cup for someone sick or elderly who is confined to bed;

— for pouring marinade over meat on a barbecue. It will give an even coverage and will not make as much mess if tipped over.

EATING (*see also* ON OUTINGS *chapter*)

When a small child first begins to eat at the table, place her meal on a tray. This should contain any spillages.

Do not add sugar or salt to your baby's food. They will be much better off not developing a taste for salty and sweet foods.

To stop children arguing over who will get which portion of a treat, get one child to divide it and the other to have first choice. They are bound to get similar amounts!

FEEDING BABIES (*see* Breastfeeding, *this chapter*)

If a baby 'spills' a lot or is sick after feeds, sit her as upright as possible in her car seat or capsule, after a feed, to make him as comfortable as possible, if you are not able to hold her.

If a baby does not want to take food off a spoon when introducing solids to him, dip your clean finger into the food and let him suck it off your finger. As he gets a taste for the food, he is more likely to cooperate.

To determine approximately how much food to give a baby in one meal, use a baby-food jar as a guide.

To feed a baby more easily:
— have the food in a cup instead of a bowl. You will be able to hold on to the handle of a cup, even if the infant's hands are waving about and you are holding a spoon and baby as well;

— use a small plastic spoon, given with ice cream sundaes or a small plastic spoon from a child's tea set. Make sure the edges are smooth. It will fit more easily into baby's mouth.

To encourage a baby to eat a new food, feed it to the child when she is hungriest, at the start of a meal.

To keep clean while feeding a baby, wear an old shirt. It can be laundered more easily than a lot of clothes.

HEALTH-CONSCIOUSNESS

When endeavouring to keep baby's food intake healthy, when going out, keep with you a crust of wholemeal bread. When he tries to grab food that you or someone else is eating, but that you don't want him to eat, produce the healthy crust. This should work with a young baby for a while anyway! (Whole grain bread is often too harsh on babies' tummies).

HIGHCHAIRS

To prevent a small baby slipping out of a highchair:
— cut a piece of foam plastic to fit on the seat. This will also help to stop spilled foods dripping on to the floor;

— roll up hand towels and place them around the baby for support;

— loop a small towel under the infant's arms and pin or tie it around the back of the chair;

— place a rubber mat on the seat.

To prevent the highchair tipping over, attach a hook to the back of the highchair and a loop-latch to the wall. Latch the chair to the wall.

To keep baby's toys within reach, tie them to ribbons or hat elastic and hang them from the side of the highchair or from the metal ring around the tray. He will learn to retrieve the toys when they drop and it will save you a lot of time and exercise.

To keep everything handy at meal times:
— attach a small towel rail to the back of the highchair and hang a facecloth, towel and bib over it;

— keep baby's bibs in a cloth bag tied to the side of the highchair.

If there is no highchair available, place one or two telephone books on top of a normal chair with a small pillow or cushion on top. You can then sit the toddler at a normal table.

To make it easier to clean the tray of an old highchair, slip a plastic cover, that you buy for the base of a bird cage, over it. Only use a new one of course. It can be wiped clean or taken off and shaken.

To make a wooden highchair easier to clean and look brighter, give it a coat of polyurethane.

To clean a highchair easily:

— take it outside and spray it with the hose;

— leave it outside in the rain;

— put it under the shower;

— leave it in a bath of warm water for a few minutes before scrubbing it with a brush.

To keep the floor underneath the highchair as clean as possible:
— use a large piece of plastic, obtainable from plant nurseries;

— use an old shower curtain;

— cut open a large plastic garbage bag. Tape it to the floor with masking tape and if it is on top of carpet, cut small holes through it for the legs to poke through, to prevent the highchair slipping.

LUNCHES (see Sandwiches, this chapter)

To save time making lunches each day, make all the sandwiches for the week at one sitting and freeze them. You will only need to add the fruit and drink on busy mornings.

To prevent children becoming bored with sandwiches in their school lunch all the time, add some variety by making up some packs without any sandwiches at all for a change. Instead, give them cubes of cheese, pieces of fruit, bread rolled up with the filling inside, a packet of sultanas, salad vegetables etc.

MEAL TIMES (see also Reluctant Eaters, this chapter and Special Family Meal Times in IN FAMILIES chapter)

To keep your house clean and to teach your children good habits, insist from the very beginning that they always sit down to eat and preferably at the table.

To keep mess to a minimum, at the table:
— use paper towels as disposable place mats;

— use face washers as place mats. They are absorbent and easily laundered.

To keep a child happy while waiting at the table for her meal, use vinyl place mats with brightly-coloured nursery rhymes, numbers and the alphabet on. They can be learning at the same time.

Always have the table set early for the evening meal. The family will be happier, knowing they can anticipate dinner.

Teach children about shapes, while they eat:
— cut sandwiches and other food into different shapes and talk about what each shape is;

— classify biscuits into ovals, rectangles, squares and circles.

Keep meal times pleasant, by discouraging bickering and arguments. Make it a rule 'No fighting at the table'. This should be a time for the family to have some healthy and peaceful interaction.

MICROWAVES

Be very careful when heating babies' and children's food in a microwave. The food must always be stirred, to prevent burns from the uneven temperatures. Test the temperature of the food before offering it to the child.

OVERWEIGHT CHILDREN

To discourage overweight children and incorrigible nibblers from eating more than they should, get them to clean their teeth straight after they have finished their food or at other times when they feel like eating for the sake of it. Hopefully, they will not want to mix food with the strong flavour of the toothpaste. (This will also be good for their teeth, of course).

Try not to get into the habit of offering food to children to pacify them or as a bribe or reward. This will encourage them to eat for comfort and for reasons other than hunger and nutrition and could well lead to weight problems.

Do not allow children to get into the habit of eating their meals while watching television. It will be difficult for them to keep track of their appetite, while distracted by television, and they will often eat far more than necessary. If morning tea happens to coincide with a television programme, let them know that they can eat because it is their morning tea time. If they ask for food before that time, get them to wait.

PLASTIC FOOD CONTAINERS

Check the lids of plastic food containers you have to see what else they fit on to. The lids of some well-known brands of plastic containers fit easily on to some round-topped yoghurt pots and babies' drinking cups. This will make transporting and storing baby's food and drinks easier.

Use margarine containers to put little snacks in for children to eat outside. The lid will eliminate spilling en route and breakage will not be a problem.

RELUCTANT AND SLOW EATERS
(see Fruit, Sandwiches *and* Vegetables, *this chapter)*

Children will often show more interest in their food when:
— it is made to look attractive *(see* Fruit, Sandwiches *and* Vegetables, *this chapter);*

— they are sitting at the table with other people who are eating. Try to sit down with them, either at their own little table or at the family's table, if they are not interested in their food.

If your toddler is reluctant to eat, it is often a good idea if they can think of eating as more of a game than a responsibility:
— try putting a glove puppet on your hand and pretend the puppet is doing the feeding;

— sing the Playschool song 'Open wide, come inside, it's yummy...'

To encourage a sick child or a child chronically reluctant to eat:
— place a few healthy and attractive-looking finger foods into a plastic container or on a large plate for her to select what she would like to eat. You could include small pieces of fruit, cheese, bite-sized sandwiches, dried fruit etc;

— if she is watching television and sees an advertisement for something that you can provide and which looks appetising, take the opportunity of offering her some;

— offer the meals to her on a doll's plate or in a very small dish. Children love small things and can easily be put off by being offered too much food;

— make pictures with the food on her plate, e.g. a face could be made from mashed potato, the nose from a long piece of carrot, the mouth from a piece of tomato, hair from chopped up silver beet and a hat could be made from some casserole.

If your child refuses his food, put it in the refrigerator and bring it out for him when he is in a happier mood or when he next asks for food.

If your child is particularly slow to eat his dinner, use a plate that has a picture of a person, cartoon character or animal on the bottom. Say 'You had better hurry and eat it before Peter Rabbit eats it!' Even though the fact that you are pretending is understood, a little game like this can sometimes work wonders.

If a child habitually takes a lot longer than everyone else to eat his meal, start him off a little earlier so the rest of the family does not get too frustrated.

RESTAURANTS (see ON OUTINGS chapter)

SCHOOL LUNCHES

Avoid mix-up over the family's lunches by using a peg for each person, with their name on it. Clip this over the lunch bag with any reminders, such as 'Get fruit juice from fridge'.

To keep school lunches fresh, pack a frozen orange or frozen drink in the lunch box. Not only will the sandwiches be fresh and fruit crisp and cold, but the thawed fruit or drink will be extra refreshing on a hot day.

SELF-FEEDING (see also Bibs, this chapter)

If a baby is continually grabbing at the spoon while you are feeding him, he is probably letting you know that he wants to have a turn with it. You may not welcome this new development, but keeping in mind some of the following ideas should make things easier!

To keep baby's clothes clean while learning to feed himself:
— make little plastic sleeve protectors to slip on his arms. Keep them on when baby is crawling around the floor and getting dirty;

— slip a pair of plastic pants on top of baby's good pants while he is learning to feed himself;

— keep a large T-shirt with you when you are out, to put on top of baby's good clothes while he is eating.

To protect dining room chairs, while small children are eating, make simple covers, like large shower caps, to slip over them.

Safety points to remember:
— be careful not to give your baby foods that he could inhale (e.g. popcorn), choke on (e.g. peanuts and seeds in fruit) or food that could get stuck in his throat (e.g. round pieces of sausage and

large pieces of dried fruit that become slippery when wet and can easily get stuck half way down!);

— never leave a young child alone while he is eating or drinking. Even a competent self-feeder could choke, gag or vomit and would need your immediate assistance.

To keep your kitchen as clean as possible while a baby is learning to feed herself:
— keep the highchair away from non-washable walls or pieces of furniture. As baby loves to play with food, she may well throw it!;

— have a roll of paper towels or a sponge cloth handy, for emergencies;

— on a warm day, take baby and highchair outside. The birds will love the mess left behind. Wash the highchair down with the hose before taking it back inside!

To encourage a baby to feed himself:
— give him a spoon too when you are feeding him. He will probably want to copy you and will gradually learn the art;

— give him mashed potato when he is learning to handle a spoon by himself. The potato will cling to the spoon and some of it may get into his mouth! Always watch closely in case he gags.

If your baby is not managing to get much food in his mouth:
— have a spoon each and take it in turns to feed one spoonful. Baby will consume what you feed her and hopefully even some off her own spoon as well;

— spread the food on a cracker. She will find holding a cracker much easier than a spoon;

— put her food in a ramekin instead of a bowl. She will be able to hold on to the handle with one hand and the spoon with the other.

Try some of the following finger foods. Remember to stay close by, no matter how well she's doing:
— fingers of wholemeal toast, rusks or crusts of bread (avoid wholegrain bread for babies as the grains can be too severe for their tummies);

— cheese cut into cubes or fingers;

— fresh, peeled fruit, cut into manageable slices;

— pieces of vegetable cut into sticks or manageable pieces;

— mashed potato, moulded into different shapes;

— brown rice made into small balls (limit the quantity for the sake of their tummies and nappies!);

— slices of hard-boiled egg (just the yoke if under a year old);

— small pieces of meat or fish.

When having to clean up a very messy baby after his meal:
— lift him from behind so that he doesn't cover you with all the 'left-overs' as you carry him into the bath!

— take a bowl of warm water and a face cloth to baby, to clean him down.

SICK CHILDREN (see Reluctant and Slow Eaters, this chapter)

TABLECLOTHS

If you use tablecloths while babies and toddlers are around, take one of the following precautions, to avoid accidents:
— fasten the cloth under the table with sticky tape;

— fold the ends under the cloth so they won't hang down;

— make family tablecloths, like fitted sheets, with elastic around the corners so they can't be pulled off;

— sew ties to the edges of the tablecloth and tie them together under the table;

— place mats are generally safer to use.

INDIVIDUAL FOODS

BREAD

To use up stale bread and crusts, make these 'after school snacks':
— make some tasty snacks by cutting the bread up into squares and spreading it with butter which has some packeted onion soup mixed in. Bake them in a moderate oven until they start to go brown and store in an airtight container;

— bake the bread in the oven until brown and crisp. Cool the pieces before breaking them up and placing them in an air-tight container. Children will enjoy them as snacks, spread with butter and Vegemite;

— toast the bread or crusts, spread them with Vegemite or some other spread, roll them in grated cheese and put them under the griller.

Keep any toast and bread leftovers in a plastic bag in the freezer to feed to the ducks or birds next time you go the park or beach.

Keep plastic clips, from bread bags, away from babies and toddlers. If swallowed, they can clip on to the intestines and cause damage. Break them in half before disposing of them.

CEREALS

To reduce the amount of sugar your children put on breakfast cereals, keep some sugar in a large salt shaker. It will also save having sugar spilt on the floor and table by unsteady hands. Better still encourage them to eat breakfast cereals without any added sugar.

EGGS

To make it easier for children to remove the shells from hard-boiled eggs, plunge the egg in cold water immediately after cooking.

FRUIT (see **Jellies,** *this chapter*)

To dry apples, cut peeled and cored apples into thin slices and spread them over oven trays. Dry them in a slow oven for several hours and store them in jars or airtight plastic bags. They make nutritious nibbles for children and are great to use in apple recipes, muesli and porridge. (When giving dried apple to young children, cut them into small pieces, as they can easily choke on large pieces, once the apple has become soft and moist in their mouths.)

To help a baby eat a banana, without it slipping out of his hand, cover the banana with crushed water crackers, so the fruit can be gripped more firmly.

To add interest to children's lunches, take the core out of an apple and fill it with raisins, dates, sunflower seeds etc. Wrap it in plastic wrap to keep it fresh.

If young children find it difficult to peel an orange at school, cut it into quarters, but not right through. Push it back into shape and wrap it firmly. The orange will be easily pulled apart without mess.

When straining fruit for baby, use a nylon mesh sieve or a piece of old clean pantihose. Wire sieves may discolour or taint fruit.

To make fruit more appetising for children, place it on the plate in the shape of a face. A piece of watermelon can be used for the mouth, a strip of banana for the nose, slices of plum for rosy cheeks, slices of kiwifruit for the eyes and segments of orange for eyebrows.

To make healthy ice blocks, freeze some of the following fruit:
— pieces of watermelon;

— passionfruit in ice cube trays;

— grapes;

— crushed pineapple in ice cube trays;

— pieces of banana that are peeled and wrapped in plastic wrap. Poke ice block sticks through them if you wish;

— segments of orange.

HONEY

To make it easier for children to dispense clear honey, put it in a plastic sauce bottle.

ICE CREAM

For a healthy and tasty substitute for ice cream, freeze pots of yoghurt and serve as they are starting to thaw.

To prevent habits forming, which are difficult to break, don't start buying ice cream from an ice cream truck in front of your children. If they have never known you to buy it in this way, they are not likely to expect you to do so.

ICE CREAM CONES

Ice cream cones can be used for other foods. Children will enjoy eating egg salads, fruit salad and other foods in a cone. This will save having to use a spoon and fork. The flat-bottomed cones will be easier to serve the food in.

To freshen up stale ice cream cones, place them in the microwave. One cone will become fresh and very crispy after about 50-60 seconds on high.

JELLIES *(see Fruit, this chapter)*

For an interesting variation, add marshmallows to the jelly while it is still hot.

To make a jelly go further, whip it with an electric mixer when it has started to set (about half the normal time). When it has doubled in quantity, put it back in the refrigerator to set. This makes a lovely, light and fluffy dessert and sets very quickly in individual glasses.

To take gelatine desserts out of their moulds:
— before pouring the jelly into the mould, rinse the mould out with cold water and spread a coating of salad oil over its insides. The jelly should then slip out easily and shine brightly;

— wrap a hot, damp towel around the mould for about 15 seconds.

Then, holding the mould with both hands, shake it quickly downwards once.

For a delicious jelly, use the water left after stewing fruit.

MILK SHAKES

To make milk shakes really thick and fluffy:
— semi-freeze the milk before mixing it;

— put two or three tablespoons of dried milk powder in the milk shake;

— crush ice through the milk shake while making it.

POPCORN

Pop popcorn in a deep-fry basket, in a pot, so that, should any not pop, it will drop through.

Children will enjoy watching popcorn pop. Cook the popcorn in a fry pan with a large wire strainer over the top. It will be a lot of fun, but make sure the children are well supervised and the corn is all covered.

SANDWICHES

To make eating sandwiches fun:
— cut them into different shapes. Remember to take this opportunity to teach 'square, rectangle, circle' etc;

— use a biscuit cutter for more interesting shapes;

— spread a little cottage cheese or cream cheese on top of the sandwich and stick little edible faces and decorations into it using parsley, sprouts, shapes made from apple or carrot, rounds of banana or circles made from hard-boiled egg white. Make sure your child is old enough to chew the foods you select for decoration;

— make 'traffic light' sandwiches by cutting three holes in the top slice of bread to look like traffic lights. Fill the sandwich underneath with red, orange or yellow and green pieces of food, such as tomato, egg yolk and lettuce;

— a boat can be made from sandwiches cut into a rectangle for the hull, triangles for the sails, and a strip of carrot for a mast;

— occasionally you may like to dip the sandwich in beaten egg and fry in a non-stick pan.

To make refrigerated butter easier to spread, grate the butter into a warm butter dish.

Some sandwich fillings, which are suitable for freezing are: grated cheese, baked beans, chopped dates, peanut butter, Vegemite, sultanas, cooked beef, lamb and poultry, and pate. Wrap them carefully and keep them airtight.

To prevent cucumber or tomato sandwiches becoming too soggy:
— place the pieces on a slice of stale bread. Blot the top with another piece of stale bread and then make them in the normal way;

— place the tomato, cucumber or mayonnaise in between slices of meat or cheese, so they don't affect the bread too much.

When making large quantities of sandwiches:
— soften 250 g butter in a bowl with about 150 ml of very hot milk. Mix it to make a creamy consistency;

— cream the butter with an electric beater and add it to the filling. You will be able to spread everything all at once.

When making egg sandwiches:
— use scrambled eggs, which will be easier to spread and will go further. If the filling is too moist, add a few breadcrumbs;

— add a drop of milk and a little butter, when mashing the hard-boiled eggs, to make it easier to spread. A little mustard will also enhance the flavour.

When making toasted sandwiches for children, add a beaten egg to help set sweetcorn and grated cheese fillings. This should prevent hot runny fillings dropping out and causing burns.

To use up left-over sandwiches, dip them in beaten egg and fry them in a non-stick pan.

To lift a salad sandwich into a plastic sandwich bag, without losing half the filling, slide an egg slice underneath it and slide it into the bag.

SOUP

To prevent children burning their tongues on hot soup:
— add one or two ice cubes to their bowls of soup before serving;

— put it in the fridge or freezer for a minute or two.

To encourage a child to drink soup, put it in a plastic cup and supply a thick straw. This will make it easier for the youngster to cope without making a mess. If it is too thick for a straw he should be able to drink it straight from the cup. Soup can be a great way of providing important vitamins to children who are not fond of eating vegetables.

VEGETABLES

If you are having difficulty getting your baby to eat vegetables:
— add plenty of pumpkin or sweet potato, which are a little sweeter than other vegetables;

— keep the vegetables moist by adding breast milk, vegetable water or milk. When baby is a bit older, he will probably enjoy having home-made gravy mixed in with it;

— feed him the vegetables along with another food that he enjoys, e.g. if he loves banana, give him a few spoons of banana and then a spoon with banana and vegetables, another spoon of banana and then some of vegetables. Gradually, decrease the banana and increase the vegetables! Who said banana doesn't mix well with vegetables?

To encourage your children to eat fresh, raw vegetables:
— keep a few pieces cut up, ready to eat, in a glass of water in the refrigerator, where they can be seen. Any pieces left over after a couple of days should be cooked or put in a 'Soup Pot' in the freezer. (Keep a 'Soup Pot' in the freezer, into which can be added leftovers, such as vegetables, meat, sauces, gravies, etc., ready to add to the next pot of vegetable soup you make);

— offer a few pieces to eat while you are preparing the vegetables for cooking;

— put a plate of chopped or sliced raw vegetables on the table for the children to nibble, if they are hungry while waiting for dinner. It won't put them off their dinner in the same way that biscuits and sweet foods will. Children are more likely to eat them when really hungry and so will hopefully develop a taste for raw vegetables;

— get them interested in starting a vegetable garden. How could they resist eating vegetables they have grown themselves?

When children dislike vegetables:
— grate up the vegetables and add them to mince when making meatballs;

— cut up carrots, parsnips and pumpkin and make them into chips;

— grate the vegetables and put them into soups;

— when silverbeet is cooked, strain it well and add some mayonnaise;

To make roasted pumpkin seeds, wash the seeds well and then spread them in a frypan or shallow baking dish. Roast them for about 25 minutes, or until dry, at 190°C. Add a little butter and brown them for another five to ten minutes, stirring regularly.

YOGHURT

When first introducing babies to yoghurt, offer them the plain, unsweetened variety. It may take them a little while to get used to the tart taste, but you are more likely to get them to accept it if they haven't tasted the fruity, sweetened ones. It will be better for them as well.

Children will love frozen yoghurt. Allow it to thaw partially before eating and it will taste like a creamy ice cream.

To make it easier for children to eat yoghurt without making a mess, poke a thick straw through the top and let them sip the contents. This is a great way of eating it while travelling.

HASSLE-FREE LIVING WITH KIDS...
On outings

(see also **ON HOLIDAYS** *and* **IN FAMILIES***)*

BABYSITTERS

When selecting a babysitter whom you don't know:
— check references;

— ask her to talk about her previous experiences so that you are more able to gauge her competence and confidence;

— observe how she relates to your children;

— check to see the times she is available.

When a babysitter comes for the first time, to look after your children:
— leave lists of what he is required to do with each child, e.g. meal times, bed times and routines;

— have him spend a little time with you and the children before you have to go out so the children can get used to him and so that you can show him where everything is, including telephone, first aid box etc.

To ease the responsibility of your babysitter:
— leave a note or tell your babysitter what sort of behaviour to expect from your children, e.g. how much Sarah is likely to cry etc. This will help her to decide if the child is in any sort of abnormal trouble. This will be especially helpful if she is looking after a baby;

— leave a card handy listing emergency phone numbers and instructions, e.g. what to do if someone comes to the door, the telephone rings, a child is sick etc. It can be a good idea to type out a note and have it handy to use each time you have a babysitter. Place it in a plastic page cover to keep it in good order. Update it as your children get older or the situation changes;

— always tell him or her where you will be, with the phone number if possible, and give the number of someone who can be rung in an emergency, preferably a responsible neighbour or nearby relative;

— make sure there aren't any dangerous substances within reach of your children, while you are out of the house. You may think you are 'in control', but you can't expect a babysitter to be as aware;

— show them around the house, pointing out the bathroom, the light switches, exits etc. Let them know if you are happy for them to play the stereo, watch television, have visitors and so on;

— leave a torch or candle and matches out, in case there is a power cut.

Enlighten your babysitter about your children's normal routines and other helpful information, such as:
— what food the children should be given, where to find it and if necessary, how to prepare it (try to leave everything prepared);

— suggest games to play and stories to read;

— indicate the children's bed times and pre-bed routines;

— suggest procedures to take if the children do not comply;

— whether they normally have the door open or closed when they sleep;

— what to do if the children wake or get out of bed.

Before leaving your children:
— try to be ready to go out well ahead of time so that you can spend some special time with them just before you go. Rushing out the door will not help them to feel secure;

— about ten to fifteen minutes before leaving, tell your child, if you haven't already done so, that you will be going out soon;

— if a babysitter will be looking after your child, spend a little time helping them become involved with one another, by starting up a game or some sort of activity *(see* AT PLAY *chapter);*

— tell a toddler that you will be back and when you do come home, say 'I came back', to reassure her that you keep your word and wouldn't abandon her.

Consider having a 'farewell tradition' which you carry out before leaving your children to go out at night, such as:
— kissing the children and their teddy bears;

— give your child's favourite teddy bear or doll an extra hug before you go and tell her that if she needs a cuddle before you return to get your one from the teddy bear;

— leaving one of your little keepsakes with each child for them to look after while you are out. This will give added assurance of your return;

— carrying your children to the window upstairs so they will be able to look out at you, as you drive off;

— honk the horn at the top of the hill.

If your children find it difficult, being left behind, consider making a tape of one of their favourite stories so they will enjoy listening to your voice after you have gone.

Make sure your babysitter has a safe way to get home. If not, make it your responsibility to have her escorted.

BE PREPARED

When going out with children, carry with you:
— two or three safety pins on your key ring. You never know when you will need one for a nappy, a hem, a broken zip or a waistband;

— a damp face washer in a plastic bag to clean children's hands, faces and spills;

— a can opener and a can of baby food, if you have a baby, or a snack for an older child, to use as a meal in an 'emergency'. You never know when the car may break down or when you may be delayed for some reason, past baby's meal time, and it is rather difficult trying to explain to a hungry child that they have to wait!

In order to be able to 'amuse' your child at any given time, keep the following in your handbag:
— paper and pens for drawing pictures and 'writing letters to Daddy';

— a pair of blunt-ended scissors and paper for cutting out shapes;

— a book of short stories;

— some pipe cleaners, to bend into animal and other shapes;

— a small amount of plasticine, in some plastic wrap;

CROWDED PLACES

When taking children to a crowded place:
— devise a special call or whistle to be kept exclusively for your family, to be used when looking for someone. When anyone in the family hears the call they are to go straight to the person or make the call back so you will be able to find them. This can seem an impersonal way of calling someone, but when you can't see them and don't know where they are, it is probably better than yelling out their name in a crowded place. Don't be too embarrassed to use it in shopping centres and movie theatres!

— dress them in brightly coloured clothes that are easily spotted;

— decide on a suitable place to meet if anyone gets lost, e.g. if you are at the zoo, you could arrange to meet everyone by the giraffe's enclosure;

— make it a standard rule, when going out, that if you get separated from anyone, unless otherwise stipulated, you will all go back to the last place that you remember you were together;

— stick a small 'name tag' on toddlers who may be too shy to give vital information if they get lost. Use a small sticky label to write the child's name in small letters, their address and telephone number on a piece of masking tape and attach it to their backs. (**Note:** *see also* Stranger Danger, *this chapter,* regarding possible disadvantage of doing this. If you feel uncomfortable having your child's name showing, it could be written inside the little handbag they are carrying.)

MOVIES

To help small children to see at movie theatres, concerts, sports' games etc, take along a child's car booster seat to prop them up a little.

RESTAURANTS

(see also **Be Prepared,** *this chapter and* **AT MEAL TIME** *chapter)*

When taking a baby or toddler to a restaurant:
— remember that there may be some time lapse between arriving at the restaurant and actually eating your meal, so try to arrive before your children's normal meal time, to save a 'hungry' performance;
— check to see that there will be a highchair available. If not, take along a portable high chair or a booster seat to place on a normal chair. For a wriggly child, a strap or some other sort of restraint would be advisable as well. If you don't have anything else, your husband's belt will help keep a child secured safely to the seat;
— try to get a table by the window or somewhere with interesting things around to keep your children amused;
— take along some food that you know your little one will eat. Try not to include anything too messy;
— take along the eating utensils that your toddler is used to, a feeding cup and plastic bowl;
— have some quiet, but interesting toys and activities for amusement.

When ordering:
— be careful about the foods you order for a child. Eggs, fish and cold meats may be fine for an adult, but they can easily become contaminated and little children are more sensitive to bacteria
— only order milk that comes in its own, sealed container;
— ask for your children's meals to be brought to the table a little ahead of the adults', so that yours will not get cold while cutting up food and organising your children.

To amuse a small child in a restaurant *(see also* Be Prepared, *this chapter)*
— fold paper napkins into various shapes, e.g. make a miniature hat for the pepper and salt shakers;
— have one adult take him for a walk, while the other waits at the table for the meal;
— play the 'walkabout' game. Use two fingers to walk around the table, up over the cups, around the saucers, and then hiding under the tablecloth. Make up a story about where they are going.

While waiting for the meals to be served:
— if baby can feed himself without difficulty, it is preferable to try to keep him amused with something other than food so that when

your meal comes, he will be happy to leave you in peace while he eats his;

— if he gets hungry, get him started on his meal or some bread from the table.

When ordering drinks, children will often be just as happy with a glass of water if it comes with a straw. Don't automatically order expensive, highly concentrated fruit juices or soft drinks. If you do order juice, ask for a glass of water as well, to enable you to dilute the juice.

SHOPPING *(see also* DEVELOPMENT *chapter)*

Don't take children supermarket shopping when they are hungry! They will want to buy everything they see. It's not good for anyone to do supermarket shopping while hungry.

When sitting a baby in the carry basket of a supermarket trolley, use some sort of restraint to prevent her from standing up and falling out. If necessary, secure her to the seat with an adult's belt.

To make supermarket shopping more interesting for a child, cut out the fronts of some packets and wrappers of items you are wanting to buy so that he can help you find them.

If your baby or toddler becomes irritable while out shopping with you:
— go at lunch time and pack some sandwiches for him to eat while sitting in the stroller or supermarket trolley. Small packets of raisins or sultanas will keep him occupied for quite a while too;

— use this time to talk with her. If she feels you are giving her attention, she is more likely to be happy;

— sing songs quietly with her if necessary;

— if you are shopping with a friend, try swapping babies while walking around the supermarket. A child who becomes irritable for his mother, may perform better when someone else is wheeling him around.

In case your children get lost in a large shop or shopping centre, teach them the following:
— to go up to the nearest shopkeeper and explain what has happened;

— make sure the children know their name, address and phone number;

— go back to the last place you were together and tell a shopkeeper or policeman what has happened.

STRANGER DANGER

Teach children the basic rules of 'Stranger Danger':
— never accept anything from a stranger;

— never talk to strangers without your parents being present;

— never wander off alone anywhere;

— never let people into your house while you are alone. Always get your parents to come to the door when there is a stranger there;

— never take short cuts or walk alone in secluded places, such as parks, alley ways, construction sites, bush tracks etc;

— when walking to and from school, always stay with a group children;

— don't linger around the school when it is time to go home;

— never go into a stranger's house;

— never get into a stranger's car. If someone drives along beside you and tries to get you into their car, turn around and run as fast as you can in the opposite direction – preferably into a shop or somewhere with a lot of people. If you turn around, it will be difficult for the car to turn around too;

— if someone stops in a car and asks directions, don't move closer to the car to hear them speak, keep well away;

— don't be fooled by the person sounding desperate and telling a story like 'your mother has been sent to hospital and she said for me to pick you up to take you to her';

— never go into public toilets alone;

— if someone harasses you, shout out 'Stranger', or 'I don't know you' rather than 'Help' as onlookers could think that the 'stranger' is helping you!

— never do anything anyone says that disobeys your parents;

— if any stranger tries to force you to do anything, yell and fight;

— always tell your parents if anyone has been acting suspiciously.

Teach your children also that these rules apply for people that you do know. **To reduce the risk of problems happening with familiar people,** instruct your children to always:
— ask your parents before accepting gifts from anyone;

— always let your parents know where you are;

— never visit neighbours and friends without your parents' permission;

— never let men or women into your house while you are alone;

— never go off with people you know unless given instructions to do so from your parents or someone in authority, such as your headmaster;

— if someone you know makes you feel uncomfortable in any way you must tell your parents.

To help children understand what you are telling them:
— act out the responses they should have to the various possible situations, e.g. someone coming up to them in the street and asking them to go with them to help someone else;

— go for a walk with your children around your neighbourhood, pointing out places to avoid, which sides of the street they should be walking on in different areas and showing them the 'safe places' to go if need be.

To make it easier for children to tell you when people have been acting suspiciously:
— encourage your children to communicate with you about all subjects;

— keep very calm when they start to tell you anything. If you show anger or fear they will probably close up;

— never allow them to feel in any way to blame, even if you think they did something wrong, or they will probably not tell you anything.

When children are in public without an adult, don't allow them to wear clothes or jewellery which has their name visible. Someone could perhaps see their name and use it to make the child think that they are 'friends' or sent by their parents. The suggestion mentioned in 'Crowded Places' above to name shy toddlers is a little different because toddlers are not likely to be by themselves. Use your discretion.

If your older children are ever left alone in the house, teach them that when a stranger rings on the telephone they should take a message without revealing the fact that there aren't any adults around, e.g. 'Mum is not able to come to the phone just at the moment, so can I get her to call you shortly?' That will usually be enough for the person to introduce himself and the nature of his call. At that stage, it may possibly be appropriate for the child to be more open about the situation.

If you are concerned about telephone calls to your children while you are out, consider installing an answering machine, which would enable your children to be discriminating about which calls they answer. They would only need to answer calls from familiar voices.

Teach a child that if **she ever has any suspicious telephone calls,** to call out to a parent, within hearing of the person. If there is no adult at home, they should still be taught to call out 'Uncle Steve, can you come to see who this is?' This is one occasion when deceiving is all right and hopefully the caller will be deterred by the 'presence' of an adult.

STROLLERS (see Walks, this chapter)

To keep baby happy in the stroller:
— tie a balloon to it;

— tie to the stroller any toys that you give him to play with.

Remember not to hang bags of shopping on the handles of light strollers as they could easily tip over.

SUGGESTIONS FOR OUTINGS

When planning outings for the family, make a list of all the places you would like to go. Work out the most suitable times to go, keeping in mind the weather, school holidays, when you can afford it and so on. Then plan towards it. Outings can appear too much of an effort, but with a little bit of planning and some excited anticipation from the children, it will be well worth it.

For a good family outing:
— take your family to a fruit farm or orchard. Their efforts will be rewarded with free samples and healthy purchases. Strawberry farms and vineyards are particularly appealing;

— take a picnic with you on a 'drive to anywhere'. Just get into the car and drive out into the country until you find a spot where you would like to stop and eat;

— take a trip into the city, not to buy things, but just to sit down in a mall and watch the people passing by;

— go on a hike. Allow everyone to carry a light bag on his back and tramp off together;

— go to a museum. Children will often find a museum more interesting than adults will, so don't deprive them of the opportunity if you are not too keen;

— take them to a planetarium, to give them a much broader appreciation of the universe in which they live.

VISITING

To keep the children amused while you're all out visiting, keep a bag of toys, crayons, books, and pencils especially for visits. If possible, don't let them use these things at home so that visits are always fun.

To save embarrassing a bed-wetting child:
— take an old shower curtain with you in case you need to put him down for a sleep;

— place two layers of aluminium foil under a sheet or towel that a baby is sleeping on. Baby will be kept warm and the foil will prevent any dampness leaking through on to the bed.

If you have a baby or toddler who likes to open cupboards, keep some pipe cleaners in your bag to tie together cupboard door handles as a temporary 'safety-lock' when you are out visiting.

WALKS

When taking baby out for a walk in a stroller on a cold day, lay a blanket across the stroller, place baby on top of the blanket and cover him and tuck it in around him. Make sure you still do up the strap.

When going on walks with children, remember not to walk too fast. Children like to discover things along the way and their little legs have to work twice as hard as an adult's!

When you go walking with a young family, choose a favourite spot to stop and tell them a story, perhaps under a special tree, next to a posting box or beside a river. If you walk over similar ground regularly, it will be a place for them to look forward to.

HASSLE-FREE LIVING WITH KIDS...
At school

BELONGINGS

To ensure children take everything they need for school, have in their bedroom a box for each child to put his or her belongings in. All sport's equipment, bus money, library books, lunch boxes and so on can be put in the 'school box' as they come to mind.

To save confusion, try to keep each child's lunch box, drink bottle, pencil case etc, in the one colour so that everyone knows at a glance which is theirs.

BLACKBOARDS (see AT PLAY chapter)

BOOKMARK

To make a bookmark:
— slip an envelope over the corner of the page;
— use left-over pieces of the paper or vinyl that you have covered the books with to make bookmarks.

BOOKS *(see also* **School Books,** *this chapter)*

To dry pages of a book so that they won't wrinkle, place paper towels on both sides of every wet page. Close the book and place some heavy books on top for several hours.

To prevent paperback books from becoming tatty:
— cover the book with clear self-adhesive vinyl;

— glue pieces of cardboard inside the front and back covers and stick a piece of bookbinding tape down the spine.

To keep track of borrowed books that need to be returned, keep a special shelf just for borrowed things, so you don't forget.

BUS FARES

To make fares easier for the children and bus driver to manage, if they haven't got a bus pass or weekly ticket, make up little envelopes containing the exact amount. Children can take one envelope for each bus trip on a particular day. Don't, however, fold and tape the envelope up too tightly as then it becomes very difficult to undo.

Protect children's bus passes and tickets by:
— covering them with clear, self adhesive vinyl;

— placing them inside a plastic luggage label. If they happen to be left in a pocket and washed by mistake, they should survive.

To keep money and bus tickets safe, sew a narrow strip of velcro inside the top of the pocket of the school blouse or shirt.

CALCULATORS

To protect calculators that need to be carried in school bags to and from school:
— keep them in a small plastic-padded envelope, available from Post Offices;

— knit a rectangle in garter stitch. Sew it up to make a case and use press studs or buttons to keep it closed;

— sew a cover for it from quilted fabric.

CERTIFICATES

To preserve your child's certificates, school reports, ribbons and merit cards:
— keep them in a photograph album with plastic overlays;

— keep each one inside a clear plastic page in a folder.

CHALKS *(see* AT PLAY *chapter)*

CRAYONS *(see* AT PLAY *chapter)*

COMPUTERS

To keep a computer keyboard free from household dust, cover it with a pillowslip each time you finish using it.

DESKS

To keep small bottles of ink and white-out upright in a desk drawer, attach a piece of elastic to one side of the drawer. This will save them spilling when other things are put in the drawer.

FELT-TIPPED PENS

To revive old felt-tipped pens, drop two or three drops of vinegar into the top end of the pen. Sit it upright for a few minutes to soak in and the colours will brighten up a lot. If you use too much vinegar, however, the colour will fade.

FLOWERS FOR THE TEACHER

To get flowers to the teacher without damage, use a 2-litre plastic soft-drink bottle. Cut the narrow part off the top, put a little water in the bottom and stand the flowers up inside. Cover the top with foil or plastic wrap.

GLUE

To stop the tops of glue bottle from sticking, put a little drop of machine oil or glycerine in the cap or on the cork.

HOMEWORK *(see* Pencils, *this chapter)*

To help your child develop good homework habits:
— select a place for your child, or have him select a place, to do his homework, that is free from distractions;

— supply a suitable working desk or space with a chair of the correct size and plenty of light;

— try to keep to a regular time for your child to do his homework. Decide what time he will be able to do his best and try to keep to it;

— make sure your child has all the necessary pens, paper etc;

— resist the temptation to do the homework for him, but be available if possible to assist where necessary. When your child requires your help to hear his spelling words, listen to him read etc, plan to have the time available for him without any distractions of your own;

— don't use the threat of homework as a punishment.

To avoid arguments about what belongs to whom, keep a collection of pens, rubbers, pencils, refill paper etc, for all the children to share when they are doing their homework.

INK

If young children like to write with a fountain pen, use liquid blue instead of ink as it can easily be cleaned off the floor or clothes.

INSECTS FOR SCHOOL

To take an insect to school, cut the narrow top off a plastic soft-drink bottle, put the insect inside and cover the top with a piece of pantyhose, secured with a piece of elastic or a rubber band. Enough air should get through and a few drops of water can be sprinkled through the pantyhose.

LABELS

To be able to quickly label children's belongings, keep a roll of masking tape handy in a kitchen drawer. Whenever clothes, books, containers etc require labelling, the job can be done without any problem.

LUNCH BOXES AND BOTTLES

To save your children losing their lunch box lids, poke a hole through one corner of the lid and the corresponding corner of the lunch box with a hot needle. Thread nylon fishing line through the holes and tie a secure knot.

To remove odours from children's plastic drink bottles when milk or juice has been left in them, half fill the bottle with water, add about half a teaspoon of salt and seal the bottle. Shake it around and leave it for half an hour or so before rinsing.

To clean plastic drink bottles, soak them in a sterilising solution designed for babies' bottles.

LUNCHES (see AT MEAL TIME chapter)

MONEY *(see* Bus Fares, *this chapter and* DEVELOPMENT *chapter)*

To prevent your children losing their lunch money, tape it to the inside of their school bags.

NOTES FOR THE TEACHER

To remind a child to pass on a note to the teacher, tape it to the child's lunch box.

PAPER

Always have plenty of scrap paper and card for your children to write and draw on. To obtain scrap paper:
— ask for off-cuts from printers;
— ask companies if they have any discarded computer paper for your children to use.

PARENTS' INVOLVEMENT IN SCHOOL

Everyone will benefit from your involvement in the life of the school.
To become more involved in the school:
— take a close interest in what your children are doing at school;
— make sure school notices are read and acted on promptly;
— offer to help in the classroom, perhaps with reading groups, preparing art materials etc;
— offer to assist with class trips;
— put your name down on tuck shop or any other rosters;
— try to be available for working bees;
— attend all parent/teacher evenings;
— attempt to get to know other parents;
— visit the classroom occasionally after school and chat with the teacher about your child's progress;
— don't delay in discussing with the teacher any problems that you feel your child is having;
— offer to do extra work at home, if necessary.

PENCILS

To name children's pencils, use a potato peeler to carve a clear section on the side for the name to be written.

If your children keep losing their pencils:
— cut them in half when you buy them. It seems that few pencils ever get used right to the end before being lost;

— keep a few on hand so they won't be caught out, but don't let the children become negligent with the thought that there will be an everlasting supply.

To keep pens and pencils together at home:
— cut off the top of a plastic soft drink bottle and keep the pens in the base;

— use a plastic cutlery tray.

POSTERS

To keep posters tidy:
— stick strips of masking tape along the edges on the back of the poster, to stop them tearing;

— cover the corners of the poster with two or three pieces of sticky tape. Fold the tape underneath.

Keep rolled up posters in good order by:
— placing them inside cardboard rolls from the insides of lunch wraps;

— place a large plastic bottle top at each end of the poster to keep it rolled up.

PREPARING CHILDREN FOR SCHOOL

Concentration

(see also **Listening** *and* **Memory Games,** *in* **AT PLAY** *chapter)*

To encourage children to take notice and remember things:
— play a different version of Kim's Game, where you have several different objects on a tray and while the child isn't looking, you remove one of the objects. They have to tell you what it was;

— after reading a story to a pre-reader, have them read the story back to you, following the pictures.

Coordination Skills

Is your child able to: throw and catch a large ball; hold a pencil properly; use scissors; sit down cross-legged; eat his lunch while sitting on the ground; make large block towers; thread beads; use a paint brush.

Desire For Learning

In your endeavour to prepare your children for school:

— try to instill the belief that learning is fun. If your children are put off by boring and uninteresting 'lessons' at home, or by being forced into learning situations, it may take them quite a while to develop an interest in learning again;

— children will learn most by being able to take part in different activities, such as shopping, baking, gardening etc.

Expectations of School

Be careful with the expectations of school that you impart to your children:

— even if you had a difficult time at school, it is very important for you to speak positively about school to your children so they will not have any negative, pre-conceived ideas;

— explain to your child an idea of what he can expect to do during the day at school and, if possible, visit the classroom while children are working to help him understand;

— in your efforts to extol the value of school, be careful not to give your children inaccurate expectations about making great friends and learning to read. Teach them that this will happen, but not on the first day!

Listening Skills *(see DEVELOPMENT chapter)*

Mathematical Concepts *(see also DEVELOPMENT chapter)*

Give your children lots of opportunities to discuss different sizes and shapes:

— select some jars and lids of different sizes for them to match up;

— allow them to sort through all the boxes and cartons in your grocery shopping and decide which ones are long, which ones are short, which are the biggest and the smallest etc;

— cut up his sandwiches into rectangles, triangles and squares;

— empty your purse and money box and sort the coins into 5 cent, 10 cent and 20 cent piles. Count how many coins in each pile;

— when in the local playground, talk about the highest steps, the tallest pole etc.

To help children understand the concept of quantity:

— make a habit of counting things through the day, e.g. stairs, pieces of potato on the plate, birds on the fence, buttons on the shirt etc;

— use words such as more, many, most, half, whole, quarter etc;

— when picking up toys and scraps off the floor, ask how many pieces he can find. Count them as they are picked up;

— let your children use different sized containers when playing with water and sand *(see* AT PLAY *chapter);*

— talk about numbers of objects matching up, such as two saucers for two cups or four knives and forks for four people;

— teach your children simple number songs and rhymes.

When your children are learning to recognise numbers, give them lots of dot-to-dot puzzles to do. Make some very simple ones yourself first and then they can get more difficult as they get better at recognising the numbers and drawing lines.

Reading *(see* Writing, *this chapter and* Books, *in* AT PLAY *chapter)*

Probably the greatest single way to prepare a child for school is to read to them. Read them stories that they enjoy, to encourage a love of books and a love of reading.

When reading aloud to children, use inflections in your voice to make it really interesting for them and stop while they are still enjoying it so they don't develop the idea that reading is boring.

To help a child recognise the letters of the alphabet, make a simple alphabet chart or frieze by writing the alphabet, using both small and capital letters, in the style of handwriting that they will be learning at school, on large strips of cardboard. Cut pictures from magazines starting with each letter and paste these on. Paint over it with clear varnish or cover it with self-adhesive vinyl and hang it on the wall at the child's eye level.

To help develop your toddler's verbal skills:
— stop while you are reading to him to ask such open-ended questions as 'what is the rabbit doing?' (rather than 'is the rabbit eating a carrot?'), 'what do you think will happen to Mr Rabbit?' (rather than 'will Mr Rabbit get sick?'). Encourage him to answer your questions by praising him for what he says and then expand on his answers;

— ask your child to read the story back to you.

To help your child associate objects with words, label things around the house, such as a chair, refrigerator, television, bed and so on. Choose a different word each day to concentrate on. You could write a duplicate of the word and place it on the notice board or refrigerator so that you can refer to it regularly through the day. Make up games using that word.

Get your child to draw a picture and then to tell you a story about what he has drawn. Write the story for him. He may want to attempt to write it too. Then have him read the story back to you.

Encourage the whole family to read by having a 'family reading session' every so often. Allocate a suitable amount of time, depending on the ages of the children, and have everyone sit around reading silently. At the end of the time each person can outline what they have read.

Recognition

To encourage children to notice similarities and differences between objects:

— play games where objects are matched up according to their colours, shapes, sizes, textures, uses etc;

— give your children lots of puzzles to play with;

— when folding the washing, give your child all the socks to sort out into pairs. They will need to be able to differentiate between colours, designs, sizes etc;

— allow your children to sort through the grocery shopping and sort the items into such categories as vegetables, cans, jars etc.

Before children start school, they should be able to recognise their first and last name in written form and know the names of their parents.

Social Skills

Children need to develop many social skills before starting school: waiting their turn; sharing; fitting in with other people; playing with other children; listening without interrupting; following instructions; asking to go to the toilet; taking themselves to the toilet; using a handkerchief; being able to dress and undress themselves properly for swimming etc; knowing their address and phone number.

Writing Concepts

To try to impart the value of writing:

— show your children written instructions and recipes on packets of food;

— encourage people to write letters to your child (or write them yourself). When the postman leaves the letters in the box, the child will be really pleased to have it read to him or to read it himself;

— explain to your pre-schooler what you are doing when you write notes to members of the family.

Before you start to write letters and words for children, find out the style of handwriting that your children will learn at school and use it now. It will make it less confusing for children to only have to learn to write once!

When writing words and sentences for children, don't use capital letters unless beginning a sentence or a proper name. Children are often taught to write and recognise their name in capital letters, but are unable to do so in small letters. This is too confusing for a child once he starts school.

PROJECTS

Keep a 'project box' for your children. Collect pictures, articles, cards and booklets that you think your children will use for projects at school. Arrange them in paper bags or large, used envelopes under broad headings, such as 'Health', 'Animals', 'Foreign Countries' etc and keep them all together in a cardboard box.

RUBBERS

To save losing rubbers, poke a hole in the rubber and tie it with a piece of string to the hole in the pencil case zipper.

To clean a pencil rubber, rub it over a patch of wallpaper which is normally hidden from view.

RULERS

To prevent plastic rulers breaking in school bags, make a long pocket on a ring binder to protect the ruler.

SCHOOL BAGS

To make a schoolbag more comfortable to carry, stick a piece of thick foam rubber around the straps or handles.

SCHOOL BOOKS *(see also* Books, *in* AT PLAY *chapter)*

To cover school books:
— use white plastic bags;

— use left-over wallpaper or buy a cheap odd roll from a remnants' bin;

— use the material from old plastic or nylon raincoats;

— use self-adhesive vinyl. Run a ruler over the vinyl as you place it on the book, to eliminate air bubbles.

To keep children's school books clean and tidy, put them in a separate plastic bag inside their schoolbags. Should a drink leak or food or ink be spilt, the books will not be damaged.

To keep scrap paper and hand-outs tidy and together, make a pocket in the front or back of the exercise books for each different subject. Tape freezer bags or plastic lunch bags to the inside covers of the books for this purpose.

SCHOOL MORNINGS (see AT WORK chapter)

The tone set in the mornings by the parents will often affect the children for the rest of the day at school:
— allow enough time to do everything without being too rushed. A frantic race every morning to get out the door raises everybody's stress levels before they have really even begun the day;

— try not to speak harshly to your children before they leave for school;

— create a happy atmosphere by putting on some cheery, up-tempo music. This should get everybody 'up and rearing to go' in the mornings;

— always say an individual 'good bye', along with a hug and some encouraging words, to each child in the mornings.

To cut down on the morning rush, have your children pack their school bags and lay out their clothes each night before going to bed.

If your child is reluctant to go to school, try to find out if there is something in particular that is concerning her, e.g. difficulty with the school work, problems with peers and so on. If you are satisfied that it is simply a matter of not 'feeling' like going, use some of the following tactics to distract her and get her on her way:
— think of something she can take to school for the teacher, such as flowers, morning tea or something to show her;

— give her a choice about something that she wears or food she takes for lunch. If you ask 'would you prefer to have cheese or tomato sandwiches in your lunch?', then her answering one way or the other will help her to get used to the idea of going;

— allow her to help you prepare something a little bit special for her lunch;

— gather up some things to take along for the art department. Being able to contribute a few magazines or cardboard boxes may help her to feel important and rearing to go;

— ask her what she would like to take along for her 'show and tell'.

If she doesn't want to think of anything, you may be able to inspire her;

— arrange to take a friend in your car or invite a friend home to play after school.

SCHOOL PHOTOGRAPHS
(see **Photographs** in **IN FAMILIES** chapter)

SCISSORS
To prevent accidents with scissors:
— provide scissors with rounded ends for children to take to school;

— if you only have sharp scissors, press the point of them into a cork before putting them into the pencil case.

STARTING SCHOOL
It can be a good idea to **avoid starting children in extra-curricular activities at the same time as they start school.** They will need time to adjust to going to school every day and some children find this very tiring. Wait until you are happy with this adjustment before starting them on music lessons, sports activities and so on.

STICKY TAPE
To stop sticky tape sticking to the roll:
— stick a plastic clip, used to seal a bread bag, on to the end of the tape;

— stick a button on to the end of the tape.

To find the end of a roll of sticky tape:
— dust the end of it with talcum powder or flour after using it;

— fold over a little of the end of the tape after using it;

— hold it over the steam of a kettle and the end should curl up.

TRAVELLING TO SCHOOL
(see **Stranger Danger** in **ON OUTINGS** chapter)

Familiarise your child with the route to and from school, even if she is to be taken by car. In the event of having to be taken home by someone else, it will make her feel more secure knowing the way home.

Talk to your children about keeping safe on the way to and from school. Make sure they know the appropriate road rules, where to cross the road, places to avoid etc. Teach them how to ask for help if required.

If your child will be walking to school, walk with her several times until you are happy that she is able to go without you. Try to find an older child or companion to go with her.

HASSLE-FREE LIVING WITH KIDS...

On Special Occasions

ARRIVAL OF A BABY

As a lasting memento of the birth of a baby give the parents a small tree or bush to plant. It will always be special to that child, who can compare his growth with that of the tree in years to come.

A very welcome present for a new mother is a card with one or more babysitting vouchers inside!

BIRTHDAY PARTIES
Balloons

Before blowing up balloons for a party, pop a sweet or a piece of dried fruit, covered with plastic wrap, inside. Finding the treat inside a balloon that bursts may save a few tears.

Older children could have a balloon painting competition. Give them a balloon each and some felt pens and see what they come up with. You may need a few ideas to inspire children who are not feeling very creative.

Keep a few spare balloons to blow up in case some burst. Tears can dampen the mood of any party. A balloon can also be given to a brother or sister who comes along with mother to pick up a child.

Remember that balloons are potentially dangerous for babies and small children:
— don't allow babies to suck or bite on balloons. 'Dead' and burst balloons especially can cause choking or suffocation;

— people sometimes make 'cherries' or miniature balloons from pieces of burst balloon, but never let children see you do this as it could be very dangerous for them, if they decided to suck on a piece of balloon;

— always have adults blow up balloons for young children. While blowing up a balloon, a child will often keep it in his mouth while inhaling deeply, which can easily result with the balloon being sucked down his throat. This has caused children to suffocate;

— always supervise children, under the age of six, while playing with balloons.

Birthday Cakes

If the cake is crumbling when you are icing it, try spreading a thin layer of margarine or soft butter over the cake first.

To make it easier to decorate a birthday cake, use a picture from a colouring-in book or trace a pattern from a picture on to tracing paper and then, with a pin, prick the design through the paper on to the icing on the cake. You can then just follow the dotted lines with the icing. You can also use marshmallows, chocolate buttons, smarties and coloured sprinkles on the top of the cake. The children will love it.

To hold candles on a cake, poke one end of a toothpick into each candle and poke the other end into the cake. This will prevent large holes being made in the cake. You can even use marshmallows as candle holders.

To make candles burn evenly, for longer and without dripping, put them in the freezer the day before the party and bring them out just before you want to light them.

Birthday Cards

To give children a thrill, send their birthday cards to them in the mail.

Instead of buying expensive birthday cards for children, which often get disposed of after a while, why not buy inexpensive Golden Books as 'cards'. They have a place inside for you to write a greeting, children will be able to get years of enjoyment out of them and they are much cheaper than most cards.

Invitations

If it is difficult to keep down the numbers of children invited, let the child invite six friends when he turns six, seven when he turns seven and so on. Once the children get to school it can be difficult to restrict numbers.

To save hurting the feelings of those who are not invited, post the invitations or deliver them by hand rather than handing them out at school in front of everybody.

To make novel invitations:
— write them with felt-tipped pens on blown-up balloons. When the ink has dried, deflate the balloons, put them in a coloured envelope and send them off;

— use a photograph of the birthday child as a postcard and write the invitation on the back;

— if it is to be a theme party, find suitable pictures from magazines or gift-wrapping paper and stick them on to cardboard. Write the invitation on the back and then cut it into a few pieces to make a jigsaw puzzle. Send the puzzle, in pieces, in the envelope so the child has to put it together to read the message.

Party Food

(see also **Jellies** *and* **Sandwiches** *in* **AT MEAL TIME** *chapter)*

To save time and to avoid breakages, consider using paper plates and cups.

To make it easier for children to reach the food, use a low table or make a temporary one from a large piece of wood or an old door.

To keep party food hot or cold, use an ice bucket. It is insulated and can be used as a serving dish.

Use flat-based ice cream cones to make serving the following foods easier and less messy for the children to eat:
— tuna and egg salad;

— fresh fruit salad, without juice;

— chocolate crackles (saves having to use patty cases);

— portions of dried fruit or other small treats.

Novelty blocks of ice can be made by *(see also* Fruit *in* AT MEAL TIME *chapter):*
— pouring water into the shaped trays from the insides of chocolate boxes. Place the tray on something firm first, to hold it in place;

— placing small pieces of brightly coloured fruit or a sweet in the water before freezing it.

Party Games

To make a Treasure Hunt, place lots of clean milk bottle tops in safe places around the garden. Foil bottle tops can be wrapped around leaves on a tree, around fence wire or around a hose, poking out from under stones or steps, and so on. Plastic milk bottle tops or the plastic rings that snap off the tops can also be hidden in different places. The child who finds the most milk bottle tops gets the prize. Children from about two years of age can participate, once they are shown what to do and what they are looking for. Make sure the children are well supervised outside. If you allow your children to eat sweets (and you are sure the guests are also allowed), wrapped sweets can be hidden, instead of the milk bottle tops, for the Treasure Hunt. Dried fruit wrapped in plastic wrap or tin foil is a healthier alternative. Keep a few extras to give to any child who didn't manage to find any!

Make a 'spider web' Treasure Hunt. Tie a different coloured piece of string or wool to each child's small prize. Hide the prizes somewhere in the room – in cupboards, stuck to the bottom of the table or stuck to the wall behind the curtain. Unwind the first piece of string back and forth across the room, in and out of chairs and pieces of furniture. Criss-cross the next piece of string in and out of the first and so on until a large web is made. Have the children choose the colour they would like and then they can unwind their way to their prizes. Make sure they roll up their pieces of web as they go!

Have a 'colour sorting' race. Provide the children with a collection of different-coloured pieces of paper. The first one to sort them, according to colour, is the winner. A variation of the same game can be used with older children, e.g. sorting pictures of clothes, numbers, families of animals and so on.

If you have a collection of egg-shaped pantyhose containers, put small gifts in them **for a lucky dip.** You will not need any sawdust as the contents of each 'egg' will be the surprise. If you can make a papier-mache or stuffed hen to sit on top of the eggs, all the better.

Have a 'pasta scooping race'. Give each child two containers, one empty and one filled with dry pasta, split peas or rice. Using a teaspoon, they have to see who can be the first to scoop the contents into the empty container.

Party Hats

To amuse the children for a while, let them make their own hats. Provide cardboard, scissors, tape, glue, felt pens, feathers, streamers, flowers, coloured paper and any other interesting things you can come up with. Have a mannequin parade and award a small prize for the finest hat.

Party Problems

To make it easier for you to enjoy the party:
— be careful to keep to a budget that you can afford. Children will appreciate the fun and games far more than extravagant food, props and decorations;
— confine the party to one or two rooms by keeping other doors closed. Cover entrances, which don't have doors, with some form of barrier and make sure that any doors on the way to the bathroom are kept shut;
— if the party is for one to three-year-olds, keep it short. Rather than try to have too many organised party games, just let them play, sing and dance together;
— have the table set with the food before the children arrive, but be sure to cover the food on the table with a cloth to stop flies and little fingers landing on the goodies;
— write down all the games and activities in the order you want them to happen, with little reminders such as '11.00 am, turn oven on, 11.15 am, put sausage rolls in the oven, 1.00 pm start singing songs etc';
— have a few extra games and activities up your sleeve in case you misjudge how long they will take. If the children are restless or unoccupied, problems can begin;
— have some other adults there to help you if possible;
— hide your valuables or make sure they are well out of reach of children;
— check with your family to see what toys they are happy for other children to play with. Put the others away.

To avoid problems and accidents at your child's birthday party, take the following precautions:
— if the children invited are under three years of age, ask their mothers or fathers to attend as well;

— if the children are young, make sure you have their home phone numbers, in case they become distressed – parents may need to be called if you find yourself spending all the time consoling one child instead of entertaining the whole group;

— check to see that there isn't any access to nearby swimming pools, ponds, creeks or any collection of water;

— make sure the children cannot get on to the road;

— make sure any garages, tool sheds and rooms containing dangerous substances are locked – your children may know not to go near, but others might not!

— check to see that you don't have any poisonous plants within reach of small children;

— if you have a dog, keep it on a leash or out of sight and outside if possible and keep it away from the food, the gifts and any young children;

— do not have fires burning or heaters turned on unless they are very well guarded;

— cover the top of the bathroom door with a towel so that it will not close properly. This will prevent a child locking himself in;

— don't give small children peanuts to eat. They are very easy to choke on;

— don't give small children glasses to drink from. Use plastic cups or disposable paper or foam cups. Have each one named to help prevent children swapping cups and germs!

To quieten the children down before they go home from the party:
— sing a few songs with them around the piano, guitar or accompanied by some recorded music;

— read them a story;

— have them do some colouring or drawing.

To avoid confusion and tears, try to have the children ready about five minutes before their parents are due to come to pick them up.

Party Tables

To save ruining good tablecloths at a young child's party:
— cover the table with a bright shower curtain;

— use a large beach towel to cover the table and absorb any spills;

— cover the table with large sheets of brown or white paper, taping the corners together so that it doesn't slide around. Give the children some crayons or felt pens and get them to draw large, bright pictures all over the 'cloth';

— use a large piece of plain plastic to cover the table. Get the children to draw a small picture and to write their names and date as a keepsake. The cloth can be used for parties each year and if the same children come back they will be amused by their pictures and handwriting from the years before. Indelible ink pens would need to be used here (under strict supervision of course!).

Party Treats

If you intend giving each child some small treats to take home, put them in 'crackers' made from lunch wrap cardboard cylinders. Cut them all to the same length and cover them with fancy paper to look like Christmas crackers. Fill them with small treats and tie the ends with string or ribbon.

Place Names

To make interesting place names for children:
— write each child's name on his own balloon and tie it to the chair where you want him to sit;

— write the name of the child on a flag, made from coloured paper and a toothpick. Poke it into an upturned ice-cream cone and place it on the child's plate;

— write each child's name in icing on their own little cake or cookie and have it sitting on their plate;

— write each child's name on their own foam or paper cup. This will save replacing cups when they forget which one they used;

— write the name of the child around the outside edge of his paper plate.

Preparations For Party

To prepare adequately for the party:
— decide whether you want the party to be at home or an outing (such as to the zoo, the movies, family restaurant, park, skating rink etc);

— send out invitations two to three weeks before the party. If the party is to be held during holidays or near Christmas, send the invitations out earlier;

— plan what activities, games, prizes, decorations and props you would like and make lists of what you need to do and when;

— do the appropriate shopping for the above;

— decorate the party room and wrap the prizes;

— write an outline of party activities;

— work out the menu and lists of foods you will need to buy.

Presents (see Christmas Presents, this chapter)

Theme Parties

If it is a theme party, try to keep the invitations, food, decorations and games in line with the theme. Instead of Pin The Tail On The Donkey, it might be Pin The Crown On The Princess, or Pin The Nose On The Clown, to keep to the theme. Sticky tape can be used instead of pins to save making too many holes in your walls and it is safer for the children to use. For young children, write their names on the 'tails' and 'noses' in case they get mixed up.

Some ideas for Theme Parties:
— Teddy Bears' Picnic (great for very young children and their teddies and a good excuse to have it in a park to save messing up your house too much!);

— a Green Party, or any colour (suggest the guests wear green, have green food, decorations, prizes etc);

— a circus party;

— a space party;

— a nursery rhyme, story or movies theme.

If you would like to have an outdoor party, but don't have the room, ask the parents to meet you with their children at a particular park or playground. So long as there is full supervision this could be easier 'on your nerves' than having a party at home. Noise is usually easier to handle when out in the open spaces.

CHRISTMAS
Christmas Cards

Get children to make their own Christmas cards, in the weeks leading up to Christmas:
— make sure you have envelopes to fit the cards before starting the children on their 'masterpieces';

— a picture pasted on card and outlined with a toning felt pen looks very professional!

— for an extra special card, or gift, have them paste a large picture or draw their own on a piece of cardboard, with room for a wool hanger at the top and a small calendar underneath. Instead of drawing or pasting pictures, they may prefer to create a collage or do some special sort of painting *(see* Painting *in* AT PLAY *chapter).*

Instead of using gift cards, use liquid glue to write your child's name on the outside of her present and then sprinkle it with glitter.

Keep Christmas cards you receive this year to make into:
— small gift cards for next year;

— to decorate Christmas stockings;

— jigsaw puzzles.

Christmas Decorations *(see* Christmas Trees, *this chapter)*

To make Christmas decorations, to hang around the house, draw the outline of the decoration (perhaps a Christmas tree, a star or a manger) on a piece of cardboard and glue a piece of clear self-adhesive vinyl on to the cardboard, so that when it is cut out, it will be completely covered. Peel off the back of the contact and cover the sticky area with glitter, tinsel, sand, confetti, coloured paper, hundreds and thousands and anything else suitable to decorate it.

Christmas Presents

Make a 'wish book', for the family members to write down ideas of what they would like for Christmas. Make it fun, by getting them to write the smallest and least expensive thing they can think of that they would like, such as a new button for their pyjamas, or one night's exemption from dishes duty, to the most expensive and unlikely present they could think of, such as a new Jaguar car, or Christmas dinner with the Queen, and then all sorts of things in between. By doing it this way, they will realise that they certainly can't get everything they would like, but they may find they receive one or two things on their list. The 'wish book' could be made out of a few pieces of paper or an old exercise book, or it could become a book to use each year, to add to the family traditions. It will be good fun to look back on what each person has requested over the years.

To make presents look good and to disguise the contents of the parcels, place them in different shaped boxes to be wrapped. The present doesn't need to be the same shape as the box or container, as you can use newspaper or tissues as padding to fill in the spaces. Collect the boxes before Christmas so you will have a range to choose from.

To wrap large gifts use wallpaper. If bought on 'special' it will work out much cheaper than using wrapping paper.

To save wasting wrapping paper, teach your children how to determine the amount of paper required for wrapping a gift. Wrap a piece of string around the parcel and use this to measure the length of paper.

Save the egg-shaped containers that some pantyhose and pavlova mixes come in. Place jewellery, toys or sweets on a bed of cotton wool in the egg, tape it together and decorate the egg with ribbons or Christmas stickers. The egg will look great hanging from the tree.

To make a treasure hunt when giving special or extra-large presents:
— hide the present (e.g. a tricycle or doll's pram) somewhere in the house or garden. Gift-wrap a container on the tree that contains directions or clues to help the recipient find it. You may direct them to 'the letter box' for the first clue and 'inside the wardrobe' for the next etc, until they find the surprise. Of course you will have to read out the clues to pre-schoolers;

— write the directions or clues, on how to find the present, on small pieces of paper and place them inside different coloured balloons. Blow up the balloons and write the child's (or adult's) name on the outside with a felt-tipped pen. In one of the gift-wrapped boxes on the tree write 'pop the red balloon by the front door'. Inside that balloon might be a message reading 'pop the green balloon on the back porch' etc; until the last one says something like 'turn around and look in the cupboard', where they will find the surprise.

Christmas Traditions

Establish some family traditions which your children will cherish growing up with. It gives youngsters a warm, secure feeling of continuity to be able to look forward to certain traditions each Christmas, e.g:
— write letters to Santa Claus;

— a Christmas 'wish book' (*see* Christmas Presents, *this chapter*);

— Christmas Eve, e.g. carol singing around the neighbourhood, going to Christmas Eve church service etc;

— Christmas morning, e.g. stockings (or children's socks) hung above their beds, filled with small gifts, fruit and nuts (don't give nuts to very small children), to keep the children amused and you asleep for a little longer. (You can make great stockings from coloured, plastic mesh bags that oranges come in);

— if your children are learning musical instruments, see if they can learn some Christmas carols and then put on a small, Christmas family concert;

— a special, traditional breakfast;

— time and place for opening presents;

— attending church on Christmas morning;

— the company you have in and the people you visit.

To stretch your child's imagination, beyond simply receiving at Christmas time, have a family project of 'giving', each Christmas time, to someone less fortunate than yourselves. Discuss what could be done each year and have every member work towards it, by donating time, money and ideas, such as:

— try to make time to visit an elderly, sick or lonely person. Take them a small gift, made by the children, some baking or a basket of treats that they are not likely to go out and buy for themselves;

— on Christmas Eve, or another more suitable time before Christmas, throw a simple party for your children and their friends. Call it a 'Christmas Giving Party' and have all the children choose one of their toys that they feel they could give away to the children's ward in a hospital or some other worthy charity or underprivileged family. They can have fun together wrapping the presents and tying up big bows. If the children are young, they can leave the gifts for 'Santa to pick up and pass on when he delivers their own' or older children can have the privilege of delivering them to the hospital themselves.

Christmas Trees

To keep the Christmas tree fresh, once you have decorated it (keeping the tree fresh will also reduce any fire risk):

— stand the tree in a bucket of wet sand, soil or water;

— continue to top up the water to keep the trunk damp;

— keep it away from too much heat;

— add commercial plant food when you water the tree.

To involve children in decorating the Christmas tree:

— get them to pop a huge bowl of popcorn. Supervise them while they thread the popcorn on long pieces of cotton to make streamers for the tree;

— have them make icicles for the tree from clear cellophane paper. Fold the paper up lengthwise and cut it into long thin strands to drape over the branches;

— if you prefer snow to icicles, mix a strong solution of soap flakes and warm water with an egg beater to obtain 'snow', the consistency of meringue. Dab this on the branches and it will harden, to give the appearance of snow;

— have them make edible decorations for the tree. They can make shortbread into suitable shapes, making sure they have pierced a hold in the ends for hanging. Play dough could be used instead of shortbread;

— make 'pasta decorations' for the tree. Cut out pieces of cardboard into the shapes of stars, bells, trees, etc and glue pieces of a variety of different pasta on to the card. Use a gold or silver spray paint to finish them off;

— even young children can make decorations from old Christmas cards. Cut out the pictures, stick glitter on the angels' halos, or cotton wool on Santa's beard, and then make a hole to put the tie through;

— wrap old matchboxes in colourful paper, tie ribbons around them and hang them on the tree;

— when children outgrow their mobiles, cut off the figures and hang them on the tree;

To keep babies and toddlers away from the Christmas tree, place the tree inside a playpen. Family pets can also be kept at 'paw's length' from such an inviting plaything, by using a playpen.

To store Christmas tree decorations, use egg cartons. The round baubles will fit well and will not break.

Safety At Christmas Time

With small children in the home, remember that the following Christmas treats can turn into hazards:

— breakable decorations can cause injury, can be swallowed or choked on;

— party left-overs, such as nuts, sweets, alcohol, ash trays etc, should not be left around for baby to investigate;

— plastic bags that presents are wrapped in must be kept well out of baby's reach. Have a carton handy to put all the scraps in straight away;

— pins and staples from packaging must be carefully disposed of;

— anything colourful that attracts a baby's attention and which a baby can reach must pass every safety test.

Waiting For Christmas

To help keep young children amused and occupied while waiting for Christmas Day:

— get them to make their own Christmas cards. Close friends and relations will love the artistic efforts of even the youngest children;

— give them old Christmas cards to make into jigsaw puzzles;

— give them some up-to-date photographs of family and friends who live near and far away to make into a collage. Attach the photos to a large piece of coloured card and write the year above. Leave a space for photos of Christmas Day, for that year, to be added later. Hang it on the wall for everyone to enjoy and keep them for posterity with your Christmas decorations. If this is done each year, it will be a lot of fun displaying more and more 'years of our lives' at Christmas time.

To help young children understand 'how long' it will be until Christmas, make an advent calendar. Cut a large sheet of cardboard into the shape of a Christmas tree, an angel, the nativity scene or some other suitable Christmas design. Cut around twenty-five little 'doors' to be opened on each day in December before Christmas. Have the number of the day on the outside of the door and a little picture drawn or cut from an old Christmas card, a Bible verse or happy thought to read each day.

Above all, have fun, keep safe and enjoy those around you at Christmas!

EASTER

To colour Easter eggs, simply hard-boil the eggs with natural food colouring added to the water. Colours can be obtained from the following natural foods:

— blue from 3 red cabbage leaves, shredded and soaked;

— brown from strong coffee;

— pink from boysenberry juice;

— tan from 3 onion skins.

For a special Easter breakfast, fill a basket with different coloured hard-boiled eggs. Use either the natural food colourings, above or use normal food colourings. When the eggs are cooked, plunge them immediately into small bowls, containing the food colouring and 1 tablespoon vinegar. Leave them for at least two minutes before draining.

HASSLE-FREE LIVING WITH KIDS...
In transit

(see also **Bikes** *in* **AT PLAY** *and* **ON HOLIDAYS** *chapters)*

AIR TRAVEL *(see* **Bus Travel,** *and* **Car Travel,** *this chapter and* **ON HOLIDAYS** *chapter)*

Airports

Make sure you have a stroller available, for use at airports, at all times. Ask to be able to take a small stroller up to the plane with you. The last thing you will need at an airport is to have to carry a tired baby or toddler and your baggage, before take-off, during stopovers and when going through immigration.

A back-pack for baby will enable you to keep your hands free and is ideal if you have a toddler as well.

If you have short stop-overs, where you are required to stay in the terminal, place a name tag on your child, with his name, flight number and destination on it *(see also* Stranger Danger *in* ON OUTINGS *chapter).*

Asking for Assistance

When taking babies and young children on long flights:
— remember to ask for everything, that you will require, when you book your seats, e.g. special food, bassinet for baby, bulkhead seats, aisle seats etc;

— when requesting help from the cabin crew, be specific about what you require, e.g. when you want the bottle warmed;

— while on board, request assistance when you land so they can organise it for you. It can be exceptionally stressful, after a tiring flight with children, trying to secure your luggage by yourself.

Clothing for the Flight

When flying with little children:
— dress your children in comfortable, loose clothing. Cardigans are good as they are easily peeled off when the temperatures rise;

— take on board a damp cloth in a plastic bag, a towel, spare disposable nappies (just in case there are none available) and toys for your little ones;

— take a change of clothing on board for yourself as well as for baby. If baby survives the flight without tipping food off the tiny trays or having some other sort of messy accident, he is doing well!

— if you are hoping to arrive at your destination looking reasonably good, consider taking a large shirt to slip on over your clothes during meal times, to prevent your clothes getting messy;

— if it is an overnight flight, dress your baby or toddler in pyjamas so he realises that it is bed time.

Feeding Children

Keep your watch set on the time of the country you have been staying in so you are easily able to work out the feeding and sleeping needs of your children.

Preparing Young Children for Flights

To prepare young ones for a flight:
— show them with a toy plane and perhaps a globe or map of the world what will be happening;

— talk about aeroplanes you hear and see in the sky and about where you think the people might be going.

Take-off and Landing

To help prevent baby's ears popping or hurting too much during take-off and landing (if there is a chance that baby may have sore ears, have a doctor check them before flying):

— give him a bottle to suck on or a breastfeed so she is swallowing frequently. Try not to feed just prior to boarding, so she will suck well at the time of ascent;

— allow babies to cry, as this helps to relieve some of the pressure on their ears.

To ease the discomfort in children's ears during take-off and landing:
— give them something chewy to eat;

— try to get them to yawn, by letting them see you yawn.

BUS TRAVEL *(see also* **Bus Fares** *in* **AT SCHOOL** *chapter and* **Car Travel,** *this chapter)*

When travelling a long distance on a bus, with a baby or toddler:
— take along his carseat for him to sit in. You may need some rope or straps to attach it to the seat. This will help him to be able to see out the window and will be safer than sitting on your knee;

— take along a receptacle to use in case of car-sickness.

Food for Children

Try to take food for the children with you. It may not be possible to buy something suitable for them at the meal stops and this time should be used, if possible, to give them fresh air and exercise. Eating on the bus will also help to pass the time for the children.

Have a store of tidbits of healthy food that will take a lot of time to eat, such as packets of sultanas or raisins, rusks made from baked pieces of bread (older children will often enjoy these as much as babies and they do take quite a long time to get through!).

To keep the bus seats clean while children are eating, take along a beach towel to put over the seats.

Take a thermos flask containing hot water, to use to heat a baby's bottle, wash baby and so on.

To make long bus journeys, with a toddler, more bearable:
— use the fuel stops to get some fresh air and exercise. If you can't get out of the bus, let your little one play with a ball in the aisle or walk around and explore for a few minutes;

— consider having a walkman for your child to listen to music and stories;

— if your child is really unhappy, try singing some songs and encouraging her to join in. Other passengers are sure to prefer the sound of your singing to the sound of a baby crying;

— have a store of lots of interesting toys to play with, that she hasn't seen for a while.

To help pass the time for older children in a bus, give them a map to follow. They can cross off each town they pass and perhaps write down a significant observation in each place. If possible, let them know where the bus will be stopping, so they can break the trip down, in their minds, into more manageable segments.

CAR TRAVEL

Amusing Babies in the Car (see Toys in the Car, this chapter)

To keep babies amused in the car:
— have a bag with you in the front seat, full of all sorts of little nick-nacks which are safe and interesting for him to play with. Hand him one at a time to enjoy;

— tie two pieces of ribbon to each side of the car seat. Attach a toy or something your baby likes to play with on each ribbon. He will be able to retrieve them when they drop.

To keep a young baby entertained in the car:
— tape some bright pictures on the roof above the car seat, on the back of the front seat or on the window for him to look at. Make sure they don't inhibit the driver's vision;

— tie some short bright ribbons and perhaps a light soft toy to the hand grip above the window;

— thread a teething ring rattle on his car seat belt so he can't drop it.

Behaviour in the Car

Surviving a long trip in the car with children will often depend on how quick and creative you are at diverting a child's attention when required:
— 'Oh look' will sometimes be enough to distract a toddler just at that crucial moment. It sometimes pays to exclaim first and then quickly think of something worth looking at, e.g. 'that car is the same colour as ours', 'there's a house with three cars in the drive' or 'where do you think that man is going in the bus?' These are certainly not the most exciting observations, but they may serve to distract a toddler from starting a crying session and if you make them sound exciting, junior may agree;

— wrap little parcels of 'diversions' in tissue paper for your toddler to open at appropriate times throughout the journey. These could contain little books, puzzles, healthy nibbles, finger puppets, writing paper and pencils and anything else you can find around the house that your child enjoys playing with.

To avoid having to look around while you are driving to check the children:

— secure a wide-angled mirror on the dash board or underneath your rear-vision mirror. Keep it tilted so that you can see the children in the back seat at one glance. Remember, if you do have to attend to a child in any way, pull over and stop the car first!;

— if you have a rear-vision mirror which you can turn down when travelling with headlights on high beam behind you, switch the mirror down briefly to look at what is happening in the back seat.

If a child is upset or difficult while you are driving the car, the safest thing to do is to pull over to the side of the road and stop, until you have corrected the situation. Do not try to sort it out while you are driving.

A small child's undesirable behaviour in the car is often caused by boredom, tiredness or hunger. When having to travel around a bit with a small child in the car, it is a good idea to make up a few sandwiches for him to eat for his lunch while you are travelling. Make sure the food will not cause too much of a mess if spilled and is not likely to cause choking. Make frequent stops for fresh air and a run around.

To avoid as much fighting as possible, try to keep the children from having to share too much in the way of toys, blankets etc. Although they may be normally good at sharing, children sitting together on a long journey will often regress. Give each person their own cushion (rather than a pillow, which will take up a lot of room and may obstruct the driver's view) and blanket and toys to play with.

To encourage good behaviour and cooperation on a long trip:

— keep a bank of 'good tickets' to give to the children when they are being cooperative. Let them know the conditions for receiving and forfeiting tickets and let them think of it as a game so that it doesn't become a problem in itself. Give a ticket, from the bank, to the child who gives helpful information. At the end of the trip the tickets could be converted to money or special privileges or prizes;

— tell the children that they must put their complaints in writing so they can be read aloud during a break in the travelling. Having to write something down will often show a child how futile the complaint is and will hopefully limit the amount of complaints received. As they are read out, the complainer may end up laughing at the fuss made over a small issue;

— at the beginning of a long trip tell them that each child can have a bonus $1 or $2, to spend on their holiday, when they get to their destination, as long as they don't have to forfeit any on the way. They might be charged 5 cents for interrupting, 20 cents for starting a fight or disobedience etc. If they are especially good they may even earn a little interest on their money;

— have one adult sit in the back seat with the children;

— have regular breaks, to give the children an opportunity to get some fresh air and exercise. A skipping rope in the car will enable some vigorous exercise on the spot or have a game of 'chasey'.

Be Prepared

It is a good idea to keep a spare car key attached to the outside of the car in some way. A magnetic box can be used for this purpose. It could be disastrous if you happened to lock the keys in the car, with a baby inside, on a hot day.

When travelling with children, keep the following in the car:
— spare nappy and pins or disposable nappy;

— a large container of water to use for drinking, washing hands, moistening cloths, filling the radiator etc. An empty wine cask, filled with water, makes application easier than having to open bottles;

— moistened wiping cloths;

— a roll of paper towels;

— plastic bag or a plastic crate to put dirty shoes and clothes, a wet umbrella or sandy buckets and spades in;

— plastic deodorant-stick holders can be used as containers to hold small items such as cotton buds and hair clips for travelling. The bottom can be pushed up for easier access;

— a rubbish bag in the back seat, as well as the front. An empty tissue box makes a good rubbish bin as well;

— a potty, if the child is being toilet trained;

— an old shower curtain to place over the seats when you pick up children who are wet or dirty. It will also come in handy to spread on the ground if you need to change a tyre;

— a bag of toys and books. Finger puppets, small cars, puzzles, small dolls with clothes to dress etc;

— an old towel to wipe sticky hands on. It will also be handy for the driver to use if her hands get dirty under the bonnet;

— a change of clothes for each child. If you are away for longer than expected or an accident happens, you are covered.

When you have to travel for a long distance with a baby or small child, keep all the spare paraphernalia together in separate coloured plastic bags. For example, keep all the nappies and clothes in a white plastic bag, the food, bibs and anything else required for feeding in a blue bag and the toys in a clear bag, so you can see what you are getting. This will make it much easier to find what you are looking for.

To make a 'travelling table' for children to press on in the car:
— place a flat tray on top of a small cushion on the child's lap;

— turn a sturdy cardboard box into a table, by cutting two 'arch ways' out to fit over the child's legs. Turn it upside down to press on.

Endeavour to arrive at your destination before dinner time, when travelling with children, to give them time to settle in to their new surroundings before having to go to bed. They could feel insecure, being put to bed immediately in a strange place that they haven't had time to explore.

Car Doors

To avoid hands being caught in car doors, call 'Hands up' to your children before you close the doors and have each child put both hands up in the air.

Make sure the back doors are locked, preferably with a child-safe lock, while children are travelling in the back seat.

Car Sickness

If you have children who tend to suffer from car sickness, keep under the front seat, an ice cream container lined with a plastic bag. This can also be used as a rubbish bin. When the child needs to be sick, get him to use the container. The plastic bag can then be simply lifted out, the top tied and disposed of in a roadside litter bin. Re-line the container for next time from a supply of plastic bags kept in the glove box.

To help prevent car sickness:
— do not allow your children to get hungry while travelling in the car. See that they have plenty of fresh fruit and raw vegetables to keep their digestion active;

— do not suggest to them that they may be sick;

— do not let them eat a lot of sweet or salty foods;

— encourage them to keep their heads still, rather than moving around all the time. If they want to look out the window, they should look at just one thing at a time, in the distance and straight ahead of them;

— discourage them from looking down;

— they could try to suck peppermints (some people think this helps);

— make sure there is always plenty of fresh air in the car;

— do not allow them to read;

— singing and talking will often distract a child from how he is feeling.

To help children who tend to get carsick, give them regular sips of peppermint tea, sweetened with a little honey, and mixed with fruit juice if desired.

Drinks

To cut down on the number of drinks requested while travelling:
— on a hot day, give each child a plastic bottle filled with drink which has been frozen. As the ice melts, the child will be able to drink a little more. It will also be very refreshing and will cause fewer spills and mess in the car;

— don't allow the children to eat too many salty foods.

To keep bottles of drink cool, while travelling in hot weather, wrap each bottle in several layers of wet newspaper and then in dry newspaper.

Carry water in a used wine cask. It will be simple to pour into cups and will be a good standby for the radiator as well.

Don't offer drinks that can stain if spilt. Even the most careful child can easily spill a drink in the car, so keep a damp cloth handy.

To reduce the chances of spills, while children are drinking in the car:
— use training cups, with lids, even when children have grown out of them;

— keep the plastic, covered cups and the cardboard frames that drinks come in, when buying from takeaway food chains. These can be washed and used again. The straw sits firmly through the hole in the lid and the cup will not easily tip over when secured in the cardboard frame:

— use plastic cups, which can be bought, with their own lids and plastic straws.

Food En Route

When packing baby cereal, for use while in transit, keep each serving separate, if possible, in small containers or sealable plastic bags. Mix in the formula powder or powdered milk before you leave so that when it comes to feed time you will only need to add water.

To protect the car seats:
— cover the seat of the car, under your child's car seat, with a beach towel or shower curtain, to catch any crumbs and pieces of food;
— spray the seat covers, carpet and interior of the car with a stain resistant coating to make it easier to wipe up spills.

While small children are eating in the car, it is a good idea for an adult to accompany them in the back seat to assist, wipe hands and faces and to watch out for choking.

Don't allow your children to eat lollies on a stick while riding in the car. A sudden stop could cause an injury.

GAMES AND ACTIVITIES FOR CHILDREN
(see also Toys in the Car, *this chapter)*

Alphabet Games *(see also* Number Plate Games, *this chapter)*
Play the 'animal alphabet' game. The first person starts with the letter 'a' and names an animal. The next person has to use the last letter of that word to name the next animal, e.g. if 'ant' is the animal chosen, the next player has to name an animal starting with 't', such as 'tiger' and so on.

Kilometre Guessing Games
To help develop your children's sense of distance, play the following:
— everyone has to try to guess when one kilometre has been travelled. If they all play it at the same time, don't let on if the first one is right. Wait until all have had their guess and then announce the winner;
— spot a landmark in the distance, such as a chimney or a farm house. Each person has to guess how far away it is. The person who guesses the closest is the winner.

Learning Games
Play a 'What if?' game. Give the children practical problems to solve which require mature reasoning. For instance, 'What if you were to

get home from school and there was no one there?' 'What if I sent you to the shop to buy some apples and they didn't have any?', 'What if you dropped a plate of butter upside down on the floor?' 'What if you got separated from your parents while out shopping?' This can be a valuable opportunity to guide your children and in a way that is fun for them.

Give the children a map, or a photocopy of a map, of the area to follow as you travel. They will be able to colour over the names of each town, river and landmark as you pass it. This will be educational as well as fun.

Keep a copy of the road code in the car, to be used for quizzes during a trip.

Number Plate Games

Number Plate Games can be quite fun. You can make up lots of different games, using the number plates of cars:
— each child has to spell his or her name, using the letters on the number plates. The letters must come in the correct order;

— using the first letter on the number plate of the car in front of you, have a race to spot something which begins with the same letter;

— get the children to make up a phrase using the letters on the number plates they see, e.g. PLD could become 'Pigs Like Dancing';

— each person has to find each letter of the alphabet, in the correct order, from the number plates they see (this game can take quite a long time);

— each person has to write down the alphabet on a piece of paper. As they see a letter on a number plate, they can strike it off. Only the first person to call out the letter is allowed to use it. The first person to strike off all the letters is the winner. (This game is quicker than the one above).

Paper and Board Games

To keep books, crayons, pencils and pads together in the car for children to use:
— put them in a shoe bag on the coat hook in the car;

— put them in a large cake tin, which can be used as a little table for writing and games;

— crayons and pencils can be kept in an empty tissue box.

To make a 'wipeable' drawing board, cover a piece of heavy card with clear, self-adhesive vinyl. Washable felt-tipped pens can be wiped off with a damp cloth.

Give a dice to your children to play 'Beetle' with. They will need a shaker and a pencil and paper. If they throw a one, they can draw the head, a two for the eyes, a three for the body, four for feelers, five for the spots and a six for the legs. They need to throw the dice in that order to draw the next section of the beetle.

Play the 'Strange Creatures' game. Give each child a piece of paper and tell them to draw a head on the top. Have them fold that piece of paper over so that only the bottom of the neck is showing and pass the paper on to the next person. That person draws a body, folds it over again and passes it on for the legs to be drawn. Look at the strange creatures that emerge when the papers are unfolded.

Magnetic board games are ideal for playing in the car.

Spotting Games

Before the trip, **prepare several different cards,** each divided into ten or twelve squares like lotto cards. In each square have a picture of something to 'spot' while travelling. Use small pictures from magazines or just write the words, e.g. 'post office', 'black car', 'brown horse', 'health-food shop', in the square. As each person spots something on their card they should call out what it is they have seen and put a small tick in the corner of the square (so that the card can be used again). All the family can play (except the driver!) and the winner is the first person to spot all the objects on their card.

Story Games

Play the game, 'This is Their Life'. Look at another car on the road and the first person has to decide where he thinks they may be going. Use any clues, such as surfboards on the roof or everybody dressed up in their best clothes, to help you guess. So the first person may say 'They are going to visit Grandma'. The next person has to say where Grandma lives, e.g. in a rest home. The next decides why they are going, e.g. because it is her birthday. The next has to say what they are giving her, then where they bought it, what colour it is etc. Some funny stories can evolve about the people in the car in front without their having any idea that they are even being noticed!

Tell stories, true or fictional, to each other.

Word Games

To get children to think about words, sentence structures and rhymes:
— each person in turn adds a word on to the sentence. The first

person may start off with 'The', the next may follow with 'gigantic', the third with 'ugly', the fourth with 'mosquito', 'buzzed', 'around', 'the', 'sleeping', 'dog', 'longing', 'for', 'a', ... and so on;

— play the 'Yes and No' game. Everyone can talk to each other, but no one is allowed to say 'yes' or 'no'. Each person could be given five matches to begin with, but every time they say 'yes' or 'no' they have to forfeit a match. The one with the most matches at the end, wins;

— each person in turn makes up a line of a limerick. The first may say, 'There once was a green, slimy toad', the next may think up, 'in the pond right next to the road', and so on.

On long car journeys, children will enjoy being able to play their own choice of music or taped stories on their own cassette players with ear phones. They will also enjoy hearing tapes of some of their favourite television programmes. If you are able to supply each child with his own 'Walkman', then everybody will be happy, including the adults! However, this is a good opportunity to learn how to take turns or patiently listen to other people's tapes on the car stereo.

Hot Days
(see also **Drinks,** *this chapter)*

To stop seat belt buckles burning children in hot weather:
— cover the buckles with towelling wrist sweat bands;

— place an open umbrella over the seat while the car is parked in the sun;

— keep a towel handy to place over the buckles when the car is parked and remember to check to make sure the buckles are not too hot before strapping your little one in the car.

To keep everyone cool, refreshed and happy, while on long car trips in the summer, stop regularly for quick swims at beaches, rivers and public swimming pools on the way. It will prevent everyone getting hot and bothered and will save having to buy ice creams and drinks so frequently.

Never leave a baby or small child in a car, especially on a hot day, even for just a few minutes, as dehydration can occur very quickly and the temperature of a car parked in the sun soars to dangerous levels within the first five minutes. If an adult is with the child in a parked car, make sure there is plenty of ventilation, as a child is usually more adversely affected by heat than an adult. If the sun is beating down on the car, whether it be moving or stationary, have some shade over the window.

To protect your baby in the car from excessive heat:
— have some sort of shade over the rear side windows. Preferably use a shade that the driver can see through, but if one is not available secure a towel or nappy over the window by closing the window on it;

— remember to use sun block and a hat on a baby who is riding in the car on a sunny day and make sure he has plenty of fluids.

Safety restraints

Enforce the rule that all children must be fitted securely into their seat belts before starting the car. To encourage children to take this rule for granted:
— insist on it from the first time your baby rides in the car;

— consistently set them a good example by always buckling up your own seat belt before the car moves;

— praise them for remembering the rule and getting into their own restraints themselves;

— if toddlers react badly to this rule, play the game that you and they have to be buckled in before the car can start.

To discourage a child's protesting about having to sit in a restraint:
— have the seat high enough for the child to see out of the window;

— avoid boredom by not travelling for too long at a stretch without stopping for a break;

— give the children some safe, light toys to play with or some light books for them to read in the car;

— do not start the car until the problem is solved.

If there is not an adequate number of car seats in the car:
— make sure the children always sit in the back seat. They must never be standing;

— place a lap belt around each child. It should fit fairly firmly across the hips of the child. An adult shoulder/lap seat belt is uncomfortable for a child and unless used with a booster seat, could be quite dangerous, as it is likely to lie across a child's neck or face. However, lap belts have been known to cause internal injuries in an accident, but they are better to use than no restraint at all. There is really no substitute for proper car seats for children;

— if necessary, place two lap belts around three children by sitting the smallest child in the middle. Stretch the right belt across the child on the right and the one in the middle and have it buckle onto the left buckle (which is wrapped around the left of the middle child). Stretch the left belt across the child on the left and the middle child to buckle into the right buckle (which is wrapped around the right of the middle child).

When fixing a car seat to a car, remember that the safest place is probably in the middle of the back seat or on the passenger side of the back seat so that you can stand on the footpath when buckling in the child and an older child, jumping out of the car, will not be near traffic.

Before allowing your baby or toddler to ride in a friend's car, check that they have a car seat or can fit your seat in. Have all cars, that the child regularly travels in, fitted with a safety device.

Be very careful when buying a used car seat and do not consider it to be safe if:
— it has been in a car accident;

— the webbing is frayed or discoloured;

— there are any missing parts;

— the buckle is able to be opened by a three year old;

— the buckle is not able to be easily and quickly opened by an adult.

If the car seat is in a car which is involved in an accident have it carefully checked for safety or replace it. Car seats are really only designed to survive one accident!

When buying a used car seat, check to see that the manufacturer's instructions are available to ensure correct and safe installation.

If you live near the sea, check the anchor points for the seat belts regularly for rust damage.

Never hold a baby or child in the front seat as it is impossible to hold on to a child on impact. Always secure the baby in his own safety seat. If there is no safer option, sit holding the baby in the back seat, but don't put him inside your seat belt.

Toilets on the Way

To give a child a cleaner toilet seat to sit on when having to patronise public facilities en route, place a deflated swim ring over the toilet seat. Keep it in a plastic bag and sanitise it at the end of the journey.

Toys in the Car

To keep a toddler's toys within his reach while travelling:
— use a bucket or a basket to put them in. Attach ribbons or pieces of tape, approximately 15 cm long, to each toy and to the handle of the bucket. Attach the bucket to the car seat and the little one

will be able to play with them, without their dropping on the floor. Don't use ribbons that are too long as they can get tangled or cause injury;

— stretch a cord or elastic across the ceiling of the car, tied or hooked at each end to the clothes' hook or hand grip. Tie soft toys to this cord so they are within reach of the children.

Wrap up some of the child's toys with lots of paper and sticky tape. When he starts to get grizzly, hand him a surprise to open up and play with.

When going on long trips with the children:
— keep some toys in the boot, out of sight, so that when a change over is made, there will be new interest. Familiarity can breed contempt when it comes to children's toys.

Toy telephones, or things that resemble telephones, will often keep children amused in the car for some time while they telephone each other and hold lengthy conversations about their trip.

HASSLE-FREE LIVING WITH KIDS.

At work

ATTITUDE TO WORK

Remember that a good attitude to work is half the battle. If children hear their parents forever complaining about the chores they have to do, or talk about their employment as if it were pure drudgery, they will quickly 'catch on' that work is only to be complained about and that cheerful cooperation is not to be expected!

BATHROOM

Teach your children to do the following after their baths:
— empty their toys of water and put them away;

— wipe around the bath with a nylon net ball or cloth while the water is being drained;

— wipe up any spilt water;

— hang up their towels neatly;

— put their dirty clothes in the laundry basket.

BED-MAKING (see also **Rewards,** this chapter)

To make it easier for children to strip and make beds, keep the pairs of sheets folded together, with the right sides facing each other, in the linen cupboard, ready to be put straight on to the bed.

To encourage an older child reluctant to make his own bed, fold up all the blankets, pillowcases and sheets and put these under his pillow next time the task is neglected. Making one's bed from scratch before getting into it isn't much fun and the child may decide he prefers pulling up the bed clothes neatly each morning after all.

BEDROOMS (see **IN THE BEDROOM** chapter)

To encourage a child to keep his bedroom tidy *(see also* Rewards, *this chapter):*

— make sure he has a place to put everything;

— try to instill appreciation for living in an ordered and attractive place;

— on an attractive piece of paper, write down what you consider constitutes a neat room and hang this on his door. This will ensure consistency both with his performance and your expectations and will give him a sense of achievement as he mentally 'ticks off' the jobs he has done. Don't set standards which are too difficult for your child to consistently attain.

COOKING (see also **Baking** in **AT PLAY** chapter)

Teach your boys and girls to cook simple things from a young age. Although the thought of it may be rather off-putting, it will pay off in the long run!
Some easy cooking lessons for young children: cheese on toast; scrambled eggs; very simple cakes.

If your children make, or help to make, their own breakfast, reduce the amount of movement required in the kitchen by keeping together items which are used at the same time. For instance, keep the bread, toaster, toast rack, mugs, tea, coffee, sweetener, kettle, used-tea-bag receptacle etc together or within easy reach of each other.

Try to involve your little ones as you work with food in the kitchen. From a young age, get them to 'help' you:

— scrub potatoes with a brush;

— polishing an apple;

— taking dried fruit out of a container;

— measuring rice or pasta;

— mixing dough;

— spreading slices of toast (easier than bread to spread).

DISHWASHING

Give your children lessons on how to systematically do the washing up. Teach them how to scrape and rinse dirty dishes, stack them neatly on the bench, fill very dirty dishes and pans with water to soak and to start washing the glasses and cutlery. If the bench looks like it is in relative order to begin with, the task will not seem as daunting.

To protect the dishes when children are doing the washing up, place a towel in the bottom of the sink and rubber or plastic teapot spouts over the taps, if they don't turn out of the way.

To save time in the mornings, fill the kitchen sink with hot, sudsy water so that each person can rinse his own dishes after breakfast. If small children are too young to wash them properly it will still save time if they can be soaking in the water.

If your children are reluctant to dry the dishes, ask them to come and dry 'seven items each' or how many you decide. If they know there is a limit to what is required of them, they may be more willing to come.

If your children like to 'select' the dishes they dry from underneath the others on the dish rack, discourage this by suggesting that they pick up the dishes very carefully, trying not to move anything else on the rack, in the same way as you play 'pick-up-sticks'. This should hopefully keep your dishes intact longer!

DUSTING

To encourage your child to help with dusting, paint a face on an old sock with a felt-tip pen. When the ink is dry, let your child put the sock over his hand and the puppet can help with the dusting.

Show your children how to dust quickly, by putting a pair of old woollen socks on your hands and wiping around the furniture with both hands. This would not be a good method of dusting around breakable objects.

ENLISTING HELPERS (see also Toddlers' Helpfulness, this chapter)

Many two- to four-year-old children will be able to: pass you nappies and some other items for baby brother or sister; put away books on a shelf (teach them to 'make a space for it'); put dirty clothes in the laundry basket; put rubbish in wastepaper baskets and inside bins; put away bath toys; tidy up toys after use; clean up after playing with most things; help with dusting; hang coats on low hooks; sort out some laundry, e.g. clothes belonging to themselves, matching socks etc; set the table, in a fashion (with safe items only); empty dishwasher of non-breakable items; help with making their bed; water outdoor plants; bring in the mail.

Many five- and six-year-olds should be able to:
— set the table; clear the table; dry unbreakable dishes; help with simple cooking tasks; pull up their beds; dress themselves; hang. up their own clothes (see Wardrobes in IN THE BEDROOM chapter); fold washing; put away toys; entertain baby brother or sister; pack their school bags; help look after pets.

Many seven- and eight-year-olds should be able to:
— prepare their own cereal and toast for breakfast; wash dishes; feed a baby; dress a baby; make their bed; clean bathroom basins; dust; rake the lawn; make their lunch for school.

To encourage small children to help you:
— suggest to them that you need a big strong boy or girl to do it;

— keep some jobs that are 'his jobs', such as setting the table or putting baby's nappies in the cupboard. This should also help to develop a sense of responsibility in them.

When delegating work to children, don't overestimate their abilities or their understanding of what you require of them:
— be explicit about the job you want done, e.g. rather than just saying 'Clean up the back yard', list the jobs you want them to complete, such as putting away the toys, sweeping the path and picking up the dead leaves;

— give 'job training'. The children will be disappointed if they feel you don't appreciate their efforts and it will save time if you show them exactly how you would like a task to be done before they start;

— work together with your child on the task you want him to do. Not only is the job more likely to be completed, but the time spent together could be valuable.

When the children are old enough to help with most jobs around the house, plan regular 'Family Clean Up Days' every two months or so. Plan it to be as enjoyable as possible while achieving maximum results and arrange to treat everyone afterwards with a meal out or a special outing.

Give your children incentives to complete some jobs. For example, they may not feel like drying the dishes, but encourage them by saying that when the dishes are dry they can use them to eat dinner.

Hand out lists to each child of the jobs they are to do over a specific period of time. They can come to you to mark them off and when the list is complete they may receive a special privilege or treat.

To make a job that your children really don't enjoy, more acceptable, make it into a game.

FRUIT-PICKING

To enable children to help you pick fruit off high branches, nail an empty can on to the end of a long stick or broom handle. Cut the shape of a 'V' out of the top edge of the can, opposite where the stick is joined to it. Slide the tin under the fruit so the V edge will cut the stem and the fruit will drop into the can.

HELPFULNESS

Teach boys and girls from a young age to be helpful. Capitalise on your two and three-year old's desire to help by teaching him to do simple tasks such as clearing the table of non-breakable items, washing plastic dishes, putting toys away etc. Willingly accept their offer to help whenever possible as this makes them feel needed. Make it fun and let them know that their contributions are appreciated. Slowly introduce some chores that they don't enjoy along with the ones that they do. Train them to always tidy up after them so that it becomes a habit.

To encourage children to do jobs when asked, play a game of 'house' or 'waiters and waitresses' with your children. Play along with them at their level and make it fun. Good habits can be learnt in a game.

When teaching small children different chores, make it fun by allowing them to dress for the part, e.g. they could wear a chef's hat and apron while cooking, a maid's hat and pinafore while dusting and a shirt and bow tie while setting and waiting at tables.

In a positive, non-threatening way, endeavour to get across to all the family the idea that **everyone who lives in the house should contribute to keeping it clean.**

To encourage helpfulness in children, have a list on the fridge or on a notice board of chores that need to be done around the home. This will show the family just what does need doing and hopefully encourage them to volunteer their help. The idea you want to convey is that running a home is teamwork! When your children are bored or are simply wanting to bless you, they can choose one of the chores to do and can sign it and cross it off when it is completed. There is something very fulfilling about being able to cross things off and if they can leave their name behind, that in itself may be enough reward. Lots of praise and some rewards can be distributed accordingly.

Write little chores on separate pieces of paper and put them into a 'lucky dip' box. They can be things that need doing occasionally, such as 'tidy your wardrobe', 'empty the waste-paper baskets', 'polish the coffee table', 'tidy up the cutlery drawer' etc. Get your helpers to dip into the box and pull out one chore to do.

Don't leave it until your children are teenagers to teach them how to run a home. With all the homework and study they have to do and the social activities they will want to be involved in, this will usually be too late!

Have family meetings to discuss work that needs to be done. Get everybody's opinions to decide who should do what. When the jobs have been delegated, don't be tempted to do the work yourself. A dinner without vegetables one night may encourage the one on 'vegies' to perform the next night (unless of course you have chosen someone who detests eating them!).

IRONING

To remind older children to turn off the iron (or any other appliance) when they have finished with it:
— get them to take off their watch when they start ironing and leave it next to the power point until they turn it off;

— plug a radio, a cassette recorder or a lamp into the same power point so that if the iron is left on by mistake the noise of the radio or the light of the lamp will remind them;

— leave a large bracelet or necklace with the iron. When a person starts to iron, get them to put the necklace on so that if they go away without turning off the iron, the chunky jewellery will remind them.

REWARDS

We live in a society where we are rewarded for effort. Just as adults respond well to receiving a pay packet after a hard week's work, so too children will respond well to positive recognition and rewards for jobs well done. As the children get older, monetary rewards for jobs well done will hopefully teach them the concept that if they want to buy something of value, they will have to work hard to be able to afford it. However, it is important for them not to expect payment for everything they do. Children should learn to do some things because they want to please and because it is the right thing to do. Depending on how well the child extended herself, rewards could perhaps take the form of one of the following:

— verbal praise and recognition for what she has done. Don't just say 'Good girl' and leave it at that. Let the child know that you have noticed and really appreciate the details of what she has done, e.g. 'You have really worked hard to clean right into the corners' or 'The shoes are lined up so neatly in the cupboard'. Even if the job is not as good as you would like it to be, find something positive to show your appreciation of;

— very young children can only understand immediate rewards, but resist the temptation to continually give out food as payment;

— for children to whom tidiness does not come easily, give small rewards for each day that their room stays tidy after a big clean up. That will mean that everything will have to be put away in its correct place, the bed made, curtains opened etc;

— the winner of a race to finish a particular job can be rewarded with the opportunity of choosing a television programme or having someone over to play;

— if a child's problem area is bed-making, provide a reward (perhaps $1 a week or a trip to the park) when the child has made his bed each day for the week. This should encourage a child to be consistent with his chores and get him in to the habit of daily making his bed, or whatever other task needs doing;

— if you are happy for your child to receive a certain amount of pocket money each week (say as an example $1.50), consider giving him 75 cents of it as a standard procedure and keeping the second 75 cents as a reward for effort. He could either be docked for what hasn't been done consistently or given the extra for what has been done;

— extra tasks, which don't have to be done regularly, can be rewarded in a special way. Perhaps you can owe the child a certain amount of time where he can ask you to do anything with him (within reason of course), e.g. half an hour to work on a puzzle with him or twenty minutes with him in the sand pit building sand castles.

ROSTERS

To teach children a sense of responsibility, make up a roster of daily chores for the children to do. Not only should the duties be stipulated, but also the deadlines for their completion, e.g. feed the cat before breakfast.

SHOE CLEANING

To make it easier for children to clean their own shoes, keep each different coloured shoe polish separate in its own plastic bag, along with the appropriate brushes, cloths and polishing pads.

TABLE-SETTING

To make it easier for a 'beginner' to set the table, draw up a diagram for him to follow and keep it in the cutlery drawer.

Keep all the plastic plates and utensils that your small child uses in a drawer or cupboard which he can reach. When preparing food for him, ask him to get his own bowl, which not only encourages his independence, but keeps his fingers out of the way for a moment while trying to cut up his sandwich.

TIDINESS (see **Rewards,** this chapter)

Probably **one of the greatest aids to 'tidiness'** is having a specific and easily accessible place for everything. Make sure each person in the home knows where everything belongs, even if it means making labels for the different cupboards and shelves — for instance, 'pens', 'scrap paper', 'colouring books' and so on or labels for non-readers with the word and an appropriate picture. If your children know that there is a specific place for each item rather than just 'in the cupboard' or 'in your room' it will be easier for them to keep things in order.

To teach toddlers to be tidy:
— set them a good example!;

— when your little ones see you tidying and cleaning, talk to them about what your are doing, e.g. 'Mummy is putting the toys back in the cupboard', 'I am folding up the towel to put it away' and so on. Start this when they are just babies so that the procedure becomes impressed on their minds;

— have them with you as you put things away and make it into a game. Ask them, 'Does this shoe belong here in the refrigerator?' 'Does this shoe belong here in the bookcase?' 'Does this shoe belong here in the wardrobe?' When you finally find the right place have the child put it away neatly and then clap and make it a happy occasion.

To teach your child tidiness:
— where possible; tell your children why certain things are kept in particular places so they can see the logic behind your requests for tidiness;

— emphasise folding clothes and linen to your children. If things are folded they automatically look tidier, even if they have not yet been put away. When you take off your baby's clothes and when you take the tablecloth off the table, let them see you fold them and teach them to do the same;

— teach everybody in the family the important rule 'Don't put it down, put it away!' Make the saying into a song or a familiar ditty, rather than a phrase that they resent hearing;

— teach them that it is easier to keep the place tidy when there is a 'place for everything and everything has its place!';

— teach your children to get into the habit of shutting drawers and cupboard doors as soon as they have finished with them;

— encourage your children to pick up anything they see lying around as soon as they see it, otherwise they could get used to seeing it lying there and may not realise that it is out of place;

— collect articles that have been left lying around and put them in a 'pound'. Before getting an item back, the child can be given a small task to do or charged a nominal amount;

— keep a 'jumble sale' box, drawer or shelf, to put things in that have been left lying around the house. The children will know where to go to look for lost property and will be encouraged to empty it if you tell them that anything that is left at the end of each week will be given away;

— be consistent with your expectations.

To motivate children to tidy up:
— if your child likes to be around company, find something that you can do in or near her room or where she is tidying;

— play some of your children's favourite music and get them to work in time to it;

— praise and encourage your children for their efforts, especially when they have tidied up spontaneously, without being asked. Don't always tell them how they could have done a better job and don't always re-do what they have done. This only tells them that they can never please you and so they may decide not to try!

To encourage children to put rubbish in the bin immediately, always provide plenty of waste-paper baskets around the house.

When children are cleaning up, pin a plastic bag to their apron or clothes to put little pieces of rubbish in as they go.

To keep clutter to a minimum:
— when obtaining new toys and clothes, see if there is something

that can be given away to make room for it;

— have one cupboard or shelf to place all odd items so you can do a 'quick, clean sweep', when you are in a hurry. The owner can look in that cupboard if he can't find his 'glasses' case' or 'dictionary'. Insist that everyone sieves through the cupboard each week to find any of their own belongings, to save it overflowing!

— try to get your family into the practice of sorting through drawers and cupboards at regular intervals and thinning out their contents. If storage space is limited, try to give away, sell or throw out things that they can do without. With these extras out of the way, it will be easier to find important things when they are needed.

To get children to tidy up really quickly, put a very fast piece of music on to play and say that the tidying has to be done by the end of the track. Find a piece of music that is really fast and keep it aside for next time you have guests due to arrive in five minutes or for when you can't stand the state of the room any longer.

TIME LIMITS

Teach older children to complete tasks within a certain length of time. They should be discouraged from taking half a day to finish a chore that need only take ten minutes. Use a timer on the stove or the length of a record or tape to set a time limit.

Rules can be made for **chores which are taking too long to complete,** e.g. beds need to be made and rooms tidied before eating breakfast, afternoon chores must be completed before eating dinner, a specific job needs to be completed before the television can be turned on!

TODDLER'S HELPFULNESS

Rather than being concerned about your little one being in the way while you are working **capitalise on a toddler's enthusiasm to help** by including him when doing some of the following chores:

— **dusting** (*see also* Dusting, *this chapter*). Let him use a small soft rag, away from any precious ornaments and preferably on a dusty surface so that he feels he has really achieved something when he sees the results;

— **emptying the dish washer.** After you have emptied all the breakable and sharp things allow him to take out the last few plastic bowls etc. Make sure there isn't any undissolved dishwasher powder left behind!;

— **gardening.** Let him water the flowers with his toy watering can while you do the gardening;

— **setting the table.** It's a good idea to keep all baby's plates, mugs and bowls in a drawer or cupboard that he can reach so that he can help you by getting a bowl for his food and putting away his own things;

— **sweeping the floor.** Let him sweep the floor with a small broom or give him the brush and pan to sweep with. If he insists on using the big broom make sure there aren't any precious ornaments around!;

— **washing the car.** Give him his own small bowl of warm water and a sponge or rag and let him wash the parts that you haven't done yet or bring out his tricycle or ride-on car for him to wash;

— **washing dishes.** Either stand him up on a chair at the sink or give him a bowl of warm water and some plastic utensils and dishes to wash. Place a large plastic sheet, towel or shower curtain underneath him to catch all the splashes.

TOYS *(see also* **AT PLAY** *chapter)*

Teach your children to put away one lot of toys before bringing out the next lot. Although it is often easier to do it yourself, take the time to get your children to do the bulk of the tidying.

When first teaching a child to put toys away, don't overwhelm her by asking her to put everything away. That will possibly put her off for life! Suggest the first time that she put away two items and then show you where the rest of them should go. This will at least be teaching her that everything does, or should, have a place.

To keep toys tidy, have a few different coloured plastic bins or cardboard boxes. The red one could be for blocks and building toys, the yellow one for puzzle toys, the green one for toys with wheels and so on. Stick pictures of blocks, puzzles, dolls and such like on the appropriate bins to help your toddler remember.

To keep toy storage areas less cluttered, have a separate space in each room, where the toys are played with, to keep those specific toys, e.g. skates and skipping ropes can be hung from hooks in the garage, board games and cards can be kept in a cupboard in the family room or dining room, bath toys can be kept in the bathroom and dolls in the bedroom.

Make up a theme song to sing when it is time to tidy up the toys. Make up your own or perhaps sing this to the tune of 'Row, row row your boat'.

> 'Tidy up, tidy up,   Tidy up, tidy up,
> Put it all away,   Or it will go astray!'

WASHING

From an early age, **teach your children to help with the washing by:**

— getting them to place their soiled towels and clothes, as soon as they take them off, in the correct baskets. If you have room to have one basket for dirty 'whites and lights', one for 'coloureds' and one for 'towels and socks' the family can help a lot by sorting them for you;

— keep a clothes' hamper or plastic wastepaper basket in each of the children's rooms for them to put their own dirty washing in each day as they take it off;

— have a different coloured plastic clothes' basket for each member of the family. After doing the ironing, leave the full baskets for each person to put away;

— when sorting through the clean washing, deliver everybody's socks, underwear, pyjamas etc to their rooms for them to fold and put away themselves.

Index

A

Address, teaching 87
Alarm clocks 52
Allowances 84
Alphabet 157
Amusing children, in
    restaurants 144-5
Appearances, taking care of 109
Apples
    filling 134; drying 134;
    stuffed 134
Applique 46
    curtains 48
Aprons 57
    painting 20
Ashtrays, recycling 23

B

Babies' clothes, recycling 13
Babies
    amusing 4; amusing in bed 48;
    at beach 115; outside 4;
    walks 121
Baby bath, emptying 40
Baby food 122
Baby food jars, recycling 122
Baby lotion 40
Babysitters
    preparing 140-2; selecting 140
Back pack 121
Bad habits, breaking 78
Bakers' clay 4

Baking, for children 4-5
Balloons 5, 163-4
Balls
    catching 5; swimming pool 32
Banana, baby eating 134
Bank book, home 84
Barbecues 122-3
Bassinet 4
    mattress, recycling 45; sheets 45
Bath
    emptying 40; fear of 41; getting
    children in 41; noisy when
    emptying 41; supervising
    children 39; winter 40
Bath time fun 40-1
Bath toys 40-1
    sanitising 41
Bathing baby 38-40
    drying 40; newborn 39;
    preventing slipping 39;
    preventing sore back 39;
    to soothe baby 79, 81
Bathrooms
    burns 43; electricity 43;
    independence 44; locks 43;
    planning 43-4; plugs 42;
    reaching taps 43; slipping 44;
    supervising 42
Be prepared, outings 142-3
Beach
    baby at 115; baby's beds at 115;
    crowded 116; feeding baby 115;
    keeping baby in shade 115;
    safety 115; valuables 116

Beach ball, drifing 115
Beach towels 54
Beach toys, in bath 41
Beads 33
Bed time
  holidays 117; preparing
  children for 52-3; routines 52;
  winter 54
Bedroom
  decorating 49-50; safety 50;
  storage 50
Beds
  changing to 50-1; falling out
  of 50-1, spare 47; wet 53-4
Bedside tables, substitute 47
Bedwetting 89
  stains 53-4; while visiting 149
Belongings
  labels 153; on holiday 117-18;
  school 150
Belts 58
Bibs 123
  recycling 58
Bicycles, safety 6
Bird cage cover 128
Birthday cards, puppets 27
Blackboards
  making 6; painting easel 21
Blankets
  cot 48; hot weather 54;
  repairing 46; storing 46
Blocks
  light 10; puzzle 15-16
Blouses 72
Blowing bubbles 118
Board games 6-7
Bookmarks 150
Books 7-9
  borrowed 151; drying 151;
  tearing 9
Booties 58-9
Boredom 84
Bottle sterilising solution
  toothbrushes 114

Bottles, baby's 123-4
  weaning 124
Bows 59
Braces, recycling 48
Braid 71
Bread, stale 133-4
Breakfast, toddler's 124
Breastfeeding 95-6
  cracked nipples 124;
  expressing 124; spilling 126
Breath-holding 79-80
Bribes, food 129
Bubble blowing 9
Bumper pad 45
Burns
  bathroom 43; camp fires 118
Bus fares 151
Butterfly catchers 10
Buttons 30, 59, 69, 72

C

Cakes, baking 5
Calculators 151
Calendars, recycling 49
Camp fire, blowing bubbles 118
Camping ground showers 118
Camping
  fence 119; tents 121; toddlers 119;
  torch 118; washing 118-19
Car seat, at movies 143
Car travel 179-90
  potty 89
Car
stranger's 146; drinks 116
Card games 10
Cardboard carton 47, 51
  recycling 10
Cards, recycling 27
Carrycot, safety 46
Carving, soap 10
Cassette tape, warning 8

Cassettes 108
   stories 9
Cereals 134
Certificates 151
Chalks 6
Change mats 64
Changing table 64
Chewing gum, in hair 111-12
Christmas tree decorations 50
Cleaning products, safety 42, 44
Climbers, safety 44
Clocks 19
Clothes
   babies' 57-8; sewing 70-1;
   storing 57, 60, 74; washing 76-7
Clothes drawers, tidy 48
Clothes line, camping 118-19
Cold weather 54, 59-60, 64, 69-70
Collages 10-11, 25
Collections
   shell 11; stamp 11
Colouring-in books 11
   applique patterns 46
Communication
   encouraging 31, 90-1;
   with children 147
Complaining 94
Computers 152
Concentration 155
Constructions 10
Continental quilt
   as sleeping bag 117;
   recycling 47
Cooking 96
   children preparing 4-5
Cooperation, encouraging 83
Coordination games 11-12
Cords, dangling 49
Cot 4, 45-7, 105
   blankets 48; changing to bed
   50-1; mattress 45; portable 46;
   rocking 48; sheets 47
Crawlers 68-9
Crayons

recycling 12; soap 12
Criticism 94
Crossword puzzles 12
Crowded places 143
Crowds, beach 116
Crusts, using up 133
Crying
   holding breath 79-80;
   stopping 79
Cubby houses 12-13
Curtains
   light leaking 48; making 48;
   net 48

D

Dancing 18-19
Day-care, clothes 63-4
Dens, making 12-13
Desks 152
Detergent bottles, recycling 18
Development, recording 94-5
Dimmer 49
Discipline, self-discipline 78
Dolls, cleaning 13
Doll's clothes 13-14, 58
Doona
   cover 46; sliding 46
Drawing 14
Dresses
   lengthening 60, storing 60;
   velvet 60
Dressing
   after swimming 116;
   in mornings 61; newborns 60-1;
   toddlers 60-1
Dressing up 14
Dribbling 87
Drink bottles
   cleaning 153; odours 153
Drinking 125-6

Drinks
    at beach 116; in car 116; in
    restaurants 145; pouring 12;
    while playing 19
Driveway safety 6
Drowning 44
Drying baby 40
Dummy 58
    breaking habit 80; losing 80

E

Early wakers 52
Earrings 112
Ears, water in 32
Easel 21
Eating
    at table 126; reluctance 130-1;
    slow 130-1; television 129;
    toddler won't 130
Efficiency 96
Egg cartons
    germinating seeds 15;
    recycling 11, 22, 112
Eggs, peeling hard-boiled 134
Elastic 71
Electricity, bathroom 43
Emergencies 141
    telephone 87
Emergency food 142
Eyes, sand in 116

F

Fairs 8
Falling from cot 46
Families, activities 91
Family nights 91
Family rules 91
Fathers 93-4
    away 108

Fears 80-1
    of the dark 80-1
    of thunder 81
Feeding baby 126-7
    keeping clean while 127;
    self-feeding 131-3; spilling 126
Felt-tipped pens, reviving 152
Fetes 8
Fighting 94
    at meals times 126
Finger foods
    for baby 132-3; for sick
    children 130
Finger painting 22, 24
Finger puppets 27-8
Fingernails, cutting baby's 109
Fitted sheets 47
Flowers, for teacher 152
Fly screens, substitute 48
Food, introducing new 127
Food colouring 5
Foreign country, safety in 119
Frieze
    alphabet 157; making 49
Fringe, cutting 111
Fruit 134-5
    dried 114; straining 134
Fruit juice 125
    tooth decay 114
Fruit juice boxes, straws 126

G

Garden, child's 14-15
Glasses, slipping 110
Glue 152
Grandparents, stories 8
Grapes 135
Greeting cards, recycling 27
Gumboots 73
Gymnastics mat 47

H

Hair
accessories 110; chewing gum
in 111-12; knots 111;
washing baby's 111
Hair bands 110
Hair clips
keeping in place 110;
storing 110; to make 110
Hair cutting 110-11
Hair ribbons, storing 110
Hair washing
baby 111; fun 111
Hammering 15
Hand-me-downs 61-2
Headboards, danger 47
Healthy food, for baby 127
Hems 62
Highchair
cleaning 128; slipping 127;
substitute for 128, 144
Hiking 149
Holiday
packing for 119-20; packing for
baby 120
Homework 152-3
Honey 135
Hoops 19
Hospital 105-7
Hot weather 19
Hot-water bottle 54
Hot-water taps 43
House moving 99-101
Housework 96-7
Huts
making 12-13; sleeping 51

I

Ice blocks, healthy 134-5
Ice cream 135

Ice cream cones, for other
foods 135
Ice cream containers 48
Ice cube trays, recycling 22
Icing, making 5
Independence 81
Ink 153
Insects, for school 153
Instructions, giving 83
Ironing 97
Irritable baby, soothing 79-80
Irritable children 81

J

Jealousy 104-5
Jeans 62
Jellies 135-6
Jerseys 63
Jewellery 33
storing 112
Jigsaw puzzle 15-16, 25

K

Keys, identifying 81
Kim's game 17
Kindergarten, preparing
child for 81-2
Kitchen, children in 4-5
Knitting booties 63

L

Labels 153
Lace 71
Lamps, bedside 49
Laundry tub, bathing baby 39
Learning, desire for 156

Left and right, learning 82
Lego 16
Library sales 8
Listening games 16-17
Listening skills, developing 82-3
Losing children 143
    at beach 116
Lucky dip 78
    stories 8
Luggage, identifying 117-18
Lunch boxes 82, 153
    recycling 22
Lunches
    school 128, 131

Mirrors 4, 10, 14
Mobiles 17-18
    making 50; buying 50;
    danger 50; hanging 50;
    recycling 50
Money
    children earning 84; lunch 154;
    saving 84
Money box, recycling 11
Mornings, school 160-1
Mothers 95
Movies 143
Moving house 99-101
Music 18-19, 52, 79
Muslin squares, making 38

M

Magazines 12, 17, 31
    recycling 49
Manners, table 83-4
Marble painting 22
Margarine containers,
    recycling 130
Marshmallows 135
    on camp fire 118
Masks, making 17
Matches
    teaching children 84;
    waterproof containers 118
Mathematical concepts 156-7
Mattress
    cot 45; protecting 46-7
Meal times 128, 130-3
Meals
    family night 92-3; heating
    toddler's 129; outings 144-5
Medicines, tooth decay 114
Mementos 94-5
Memory games 17
Microwaves 129
Milk 123-4
Milk shakes 136

N

Nail polish brushes, recycling 21
Name tags 63-4
    on children 143
Naming plastic plates 117
Nappies
    changing 64-5; disposable 65-6;
    drying 66; hanging on line 66;
    recycling 67; stains 67-8;
    washing 68
Nappy bag 66-7
Nappy buckets 67
Nappy liners 67
Nappy rash 67
Nappy sterilising solution,
    bath toys 41
Naps, day-time 51-2
Negatives 102
Newborns 104-5
    dressing 60-1; security 45
Nibbles 138
Nighties 69-70
Notice boards
    making 49
Nylon net balls, for baby 4

O

Odours
   baby's bottle 123;
   drink bottles 153
Oranges 135
Organisation 97-8
Outings, being prepared 142-3
Outside clocks 19
   hot weather 19; play 19
Overalls 68-9
Overseas trip, with children 119
Overweight children 129

P

PVC pipe, recycling 6
Pacifying 129
Packing, for holiday 119-20
Paddling pool
   as bed 115; at beach 115;
   safety 19-20
Paint brushes, recycling 20-1
Paint containers 22-3
Paint, substitute for 23
Painting
   blowing 22; encouraging 21;
   finger 22; marble 22; portraits
   24; preparing for 24;
   with water 23
Paintings
   displaying 25; storing 25;
   surprise 25; utilising 25
Paints 22-3
Pants, long 63
Paper
   scrap 154; for painting 23
Papier mâché 25-6
Passionfruit 134
Pasta 33
Paste 26
Paste brushes, recycling 21
Pasting 11

Patty tins, recycling 22
Pencils 154-5
Photographing children 102
Photographs
   displaying 49, 101;
   duplicates 101; family 49;
   frieze 49; labelling 101-2;
   making into books 7;
   school 103; slides 103
Picnic
   food 120; tablecloth 120
Pierced ears, sore 112
Pineapple 135
Pipe cleaners 9, 143
Planetarium 148
Planning children's activities 97-8
Plastic pants 69
Plastic plates, naming 117
Play dough 26
Play mat 26
Play
   adult involvement 3;
   baby spoiling 4; outside 19
Playing in bath 40-1
Playpen 3, 123
   as cot 117; older children 4;
   outside 27
Pocket money 84
Pole tennis 27
Popcorn 136
Portraits, painting 24
Posters 155
Posting 27
Potatoes, camp fire 118
Potty training, car travel 89
Pre-school, preparing child for 81-2
Preparing for new baby 98, 104-5
Presents, wrapping paper 25
Printing 24
   vegetables 24
Problem solving 84-5
Projects, school 159
Puppets
   finger 27-8; for bath 40

Puzzles
jigsaw 15-16, 25; crossword 12
Pyjamas 69-70

Q
Quilt
protecting 46;
sliding 46

R
Raincoats 70
recycling 20
Raisins 145
Razor blades, disposing 42
Reading 157-8
stories 7-9
Recycling
ashtrays 23; babies' clothes 13;
baby food jars 122; bassinet
matress 45; bibs 58; boxes 10;
braces 48; calendars 49;
cardboard boxes 13; children's
brooms 9; christmas tree
decorations 50; continental
quilt 47; crayons 12; detergent
bottles 18; deodorant bottles
121; dressing-up clothes 14; egg
cartons 11, 22, 112; food
packets 30; greeting cards 27;
for collages 10; ice cube
trays 22; magazines 49;
mobiles 50; money box 11; nail
polish brushes 21; nappies 67;
objects for children's
constructions 10; objects for
musical instruments 18; objects

for painting 20; PVC
pipe, 6, 10; paint brushes 20;
paste brushes 21; patty tins 22;
raincoats 20; roller blind 6;
shower cap 6; shower
curtains 46, 120, 149; socks 5;
sterilising solution 123; tennis
rackets 10; tissue boxes 27;
toothbrushes 21; training
cups 126
Relaxation 98
Relaxing children 79-80
Reluctant eaters 130-1
Reminders 85
Rest time 51-2
Restaurant, amusing
children 144-5
Restless sleepers 52-3, 47
cold weather 54
Rewards 78
food 129
Rickrack 71
Road rules 6
Roller skates 28
Routines 142
bed time 52
Rubbers 159
Rulers 159
Rules 91

S
Safety pins 64
beach 116
Salads, in lunch boxes 138
Salt, adding 126
Sand
from beach 116-17; in baby's
eye 116
Sandals 74
Sandpits 28-30

Sandwiches 136-7
    egg 137; freezing 136; fun 128;
    large quantities 137;
    left-over 137; salad 137;
    soggy 137; toasted 137
Sausages 122
    camp fires 118
Saving money 84
School
    bags 159; belongings 150;
    books 159-60; expectations
    of 156; lunches 131;
    mornings 160-1; parents'
    involvement 154;
    photographs 103; preparing
    children for 155-9; projects 159;
    starting 161-2; travelling
    to 161-2; walking to 146-7
Scissors 161
Scrap book 12, 25
Scribbling, on walls 6
Security
    blankets 85; newborns 45
Self-dressing 61
Self-esteem 103-4
Self-feeding
    encouraging 132; finger
    foods 132; keeping clean 131;
    safety 131
Sewing 30, 98-9
    children's clothes 70-1
Sewing machine, teaching to
    use 30
Shade making 19
Shadows 19
Shampoo
    in eyes 39; out of eyes 111;
    preventing wastage 111
Sharing toys 35
Shaving cream, play 30
Shawls 71
Sheets
    bassinet 45; fitted 47; plastic 53
Shell collections 11

Shirts 72
Shoes
    babies' 72; canvas 72;
    cleaning 72-3; laces 74;
    new 73-4; sandals 74; storing 74;
    wet 74
Shopping
    list 86; with children 145
Shops, playing at 30-1
Shower curtain
    bedwetting 149;
    recycling 46, 120
Showers, camping ground 118
Sibling
    rivalry 104-5; fighting 94
Sick child, food & drinks 130
Sickness, mothers 99
Singing 18
Skateboards 31
Skirts 75
Sleeping bag
    as quilt 47; substitute for 117
Slides 31
Slipping in bath 44
Smothering 50
Soap
    carving 10; crayons 12
Social skills 158
Sock
    balls 5; odd 75; recycling 5, 76
Soft toys 34
Songs 18-19
Soup
    burning 137; drinking 137
Speech
    games 31; faltering 86
Spilling after feeds 126
Stains
    bed-wetting 54; nappies 67-8
Stamp collecting 11
Stamp pad, making 24
Sterilising solution, recycling 123
Sticky tape 161
Stilts 31

Stories 7-9, 53
Story times, family 93
Stranger danger 146-8
Straws 9, 125-6
Strollers 148
Sugar, adding 126
Sultanas 145
Sun hats 76
Sun, walking 121
Suntan lotion, applying 121
Supermarket shopping, with
. children 145
Supermarket trolley 145
Suitcase 117-18
Swimming
    babies 31-2; goggles 111;
    on holiday 117; pool balls 32;
    safety 19-20; toddlers 31-2
Swings 32-3

T

Table manners, teaching 83-4
Tablecloth
    picnic 120; safety 133
Talk, learning to 86
Tantrums 79-80
Teacher
    flowers for 152; notes for 154
Teeth
    developing 86; knocked
    out 112-13
Teeth cleaning
    babies' 113; to discourage
    over-eating 129
Teething relief 86
Telephone 99, 141
    bathing baby 38;
    emergencies 87;
    suspicious calls 147
Telephone number
    on toddler 143; teaching 87

Television 83, 107, 129
Tennis pole 27
Tennis rackets, recycling 10
Tents
    guy ropes 121; identifying 121
Threading 33
Thumb-sucking, discouraging 88
Time, developing concept of 88
Toilet
    at night 44; climbing on 44;
    danger 44; independence 44;
    safety 44; training 88
Toilet roll, pulling off paper 44
Tooth decay, avoiding 114
Toothbrushes 42
    freshening 114; recycling 21
Toothpaste, babies' 113
Torch
    camping 118; naming 118
Touching games 33
Towel rail, too high 42
Towels, children's 42
Toys
    age suitability 34; babies' 4;
    bath 40; boredom with 33;
    buying 34; cleaning 34;
    in cot 48; paddling pool 19;
    safety 36; sharing 35;
    soft 34, 48; storing 35
Training cups 126
    recycling 126
Tramping, safety 121
Trampolines 36
Travelling
    to school 161; children by
    themselves 117
Treats, dividing 126

U

Under-blanket 47

V

Valance, substitute for 47
Valuables, at beach 116
Vegetables 138
    babies 138; printing with 24;
    raw 138; won't eat 138
Velvet dresses 60
Videos 107
Visiting, bedwetting 149

W

Walks
    cold days 149; with babies 121
Wall hangings 49
Walls, scribbling 6
Wardrobes 50
Washing
    on holiday 121; while
    camping 119
Washing dishes 5
Watches 112

Water
    encourage drinking 125;
    fascination 44; on face 41
Water play 19, 31
Waterbeds, danger 50
Watermelon 134
Weaning off bottle 124
Wetting bed 89
Winter, see cold weather 59
Winter, bath 40
Woollens 77
Wrapping paper 25
Writing 158

Y

Yoghurt 139, frozen 135

Z

Zips 46, 77